Much happiness!

Eileen Wayne

Pilar Wayne's
FAVORITE AND FABULOUS
RECIPES

Published by PAX Publishing Company
1599 Superior, Costa Mesa, California 92627

Library of Congress Catalog Number: 82-62127

Cover photo and all inside color photos by Ray Handy.

Price $10.95 plus applicable sales tax.

PRINTED IN THE UNITED STATES OF AMERICA.

I dedicate this book to Duke and our three precious children;
Aissa, Ethan and Marisa.

I especially want to say thank you to those whose recipes were delicious enough to share.

My deepest appreciation to my sisters Nani, Josephine and Carmen, to Florence's ability and tremendous patience, to Feli, Fausto, Angela and Consuelo, who taught me so much, and to Ray, Link, Kathy, Velma, Lori, Fred, Merv, Derrick and Coy for their continuous support and encouragement.

And, to my children for testing the recipes and being my most severe critics.

Preface

Pilar Wayne was born and raised in Lima, Peru, South America, daughter of Carmela and Miguel Angel Pallete, her father was a Peruvian Congressman.

In 1952, Sol Lesser was looking for a Peruvian girl to play the lead in a motion picture called, "The Lost Emeralds of Illatica." Out of the many girls tested, Pilar won the lead. This immediately led to a second American film called "Green Hell." During the filming of this movie, which took place in the jungles of the Amazon River, the company was visited by motion picture star John Wayne, who was looking for locations for a movie called "The Alamo," later filmed in Bracketville, Texas. He was invited by the Peruvian company, not only to watch them work, but also to dine with them, and was seated next to their leading lady.

It was in 1953 that Pilar came to Los Angeles to dub the film in English, when she ran into John Wayne for the second time. A year later, as the sun set in Kona, Hawaii, they exchanged their vows and became husband and wife.

Pilar retired from her motion picture career to dedicate herself completely to being wife and mother. During the next ten years of their marriage, they traveled extensively to practically every corner of the world, usually on location for Mr. Wayne's many films, and were blessed with three lovely children, Aissa Maria, John Ethan, and Marisa Carmela. In 1965, they decided they wanted to live near the ocean and close to their yacht. They moved to Newport Beach, California. Wayne kept up his hectic schedule, making movies, and Pilar found it difficult for her to travel with him, and at the same time take care of home and children. In 1976, they agreed to a friendly separation. Shortly afterwards. Mr. Wayne left for London to film "Brannigan." A month later, Wayne invited Pilar to visit him with the children. They decided to go back together upon his return to Newport Beach. This never happened. Shortly after Wayne returned home, he left for Oregon to film "Rooster Cogburn" with Katherine Hepburn.

The children grew up fast, and Pilar decided to do something she had always had a great love for — to become an Interior Designer. She found it necessary to find a location to work from, and rented a studio inside the Fernleaf Courtyard. The place was so charming that she could entertain her clients outdoors with coffee and finger sandwiches and found herself, one year later, with a full-time, elegant restaurant. Wayne visited her occasionally and was proud of her undertaking. Neither of them ever filed for a legal separation or wanted a divorce.

After a long and painful illness, John Wayne passed away on June 11, 1979, leaving behind his seven children and his widow Pilar. She is still completely dedicated to her children. Marisa, the youngest, still in her teens and daughter Aissa just gave birth to Pilar's first grandchild and John Wayne's twenty-second.

Foreword

When I think about it, my love for cooking goes way back to my childhood. I would beg my mother to give our cook the night off so that I could do the cooking. I vividly remember the happy hours spent around our table at home. My father, my mother, and we five children had such a happy time together. My father's background was French and Spanish. What a combination! He had a tremendous sense of humor, and his delight was to make us hysterical with laughter from his stories and his anecdotes. Whereas my mother would eat like a bird, my father would treasure every morsel of food.

After my childhood years and my marriage to John Wayne, my real interest in cooking started to grow. Wow! There was so much to learn.

I was quite a young bride and really inexperienced in the art of entertaining. All of a sudden, in 1954, I found myself with the tremendous responsibility of having not only to entertain but also to be entertained by people who knew the art almost to perfection.

Then, years later I became a restauranteur in the most unexpected way, In 1977, while I was doing interior design, I rented a studio inside the charming "Fernleaf Courtyard" in Corona Del Mar. Set around an open space were small specialty shops. After working inside the studio day after day, I thought how nice it would be to serve our clients coffee and little finger sandwiches outside under cute little umbrellas. This went very well, but, not satisfied with a good thing, we started adding soft drinks and several other kinds of sandwiches.

Next, we began to offer specialties of the day. Then we decided that we just had to have a beer and wine license. About the same time, the shop across from us vacated. I thought that it would make the cutest, little restaurant ever!

The room was charming. It had a high ceiling and a fireplace. I upholstered all the walls in the softest peach, and all the booths and chairs in dark green velvet. I also mirrored part of the walls and the entire ceiling to make the room look bigger. We added two oversized chandeliers and completely covered the place with lush greenery. Well, if I must say so myself, it turned out quite cozy and elegant, and the "Fernleaf Caffe" was born.

Now, then, I am in the restaurant business up to my ears, and I'm enjoying every minute of it. As one thing lead to another, we drew a liquor license in the lottery. The "Fernleaf" did become very demanding, but it was an exciting challenge.

Don't for a moment think that everything was "sugar and spice and everything nice". Owning a restaurant is a gratifying but endless job. Every day would bring a new surprise. One day your employees think that you are the greatest, and the next day, the chef and waitress are fighting, and they hate you for not firing the other. The next day, "who stole the silver?" and then the next day after that, "Mrs. Wayne, my assistant is drunk!" Sometimes I felt like the mother of twenty bratty kids.

I must say, however, I was extremely lucky with my personnel. With the exception of a few, I had a wonderful relationship with my employees. They even stood by me and did not complain when I used to get caught doing the cooking in between chefs.

By the way, talking about in between chefs, I will never forget our first Mothers' Day at the "Fernleaf". Again, I had no chef. I decided that there was nothing to a simple menu that consisted of roast turkey, Mom's fabulous dressing, gravy, and for starters, my delicious beef broth and salad. I had been told that Mothers' Day was one of the busiest days in the restaurant business, so I made up my mind to keep the "Fernleaf" open that day — chef or no chef. I thought I will do it myself. What a perfect chance. What an experience. "Top Chef" for the day, Boy, I felt so high with excitement, It was like I was opening on Broadway!

I talked it over with my children who wanted to treat me to a nice dinner, either at home or at some restaurant. I explained to them that business came before pleasure, and they very nicely agreed. We decided that we would dine together after the last sitting.

Well, the reservations started to pour in, and in a matter of days, we had five complete turn-overs, the first starting at 3:00 p.m.. But, I had made a drastic mistake, I was only allowing one and a half hours for each sitting. I realized, trembling with fear that it took the first sitting almost an hour to drink their cocktails alone! By 5:30, the second sitting, there was a crowd of people at my window acting like chimpanzees waiting to be fed. In panic, I ran to the telephone and was lucky enough to reach my dear friends Barbara Burnett and Tom Sutherland, and also my daughter Marisa and my son Ethan. They all came to my rescue.

By the third sitting, my customers had no idea what was going on. The minute they ordered their cocktails, there also came their soup or salad. They had no longer started on these when their turkey was served. By the end of the fifth sitting, all of our feet were practically bleeding, and every bone in our bodies was aching.

After all of our customers were gone, we were able to sit down, relax, and enjoy our own dinner. We were too tired to eat, but nothing could stop us from recalling the previous hours and just roaring with laughter at my own stupidity. Well, I learned my lesson the hard way. In the following years, we allowed our customers three hours for the evening meal.

Today, I feel happiness at its peak when I have a sit-down dinner at home with my three children and friends. There are always jokes and laughter, and it brings all of us so much closer together. Even my pet parrot "Gucci" who has his beautiful brass cage in the living room on which the door is never closed, flies down and waddles to the dining room and joins in the laughter.

Putting this book together is the result of almost five years in the restaurant business. Most of the recipes I have either obtained while operating the restaurant or while entertaining during the years. I am thrilled to share them with you and want you to understand that I don't claim to be an Escoffier or a Julia Child. I like cooking and love to eat. I hope you enjoy this book as much as I enjoyed putting it together and will forgive my Latin American attitude to the English language.

Conversion Table American/Metric

DRY MEASURMENTS

Ounces	Grams	Grams	Ounces
1	28.35	1	0.035
2	56.70	2	0.07
3	85.05	3	0.11
4	113.40	4	0.14
5	141.75	5	0.18
6	170.10	6	0.21
7	198.45	7	0.25
8	226.80	8	0.28
9	255.15	9	0.32
10	283.50	10	0.35
11	311.85	11	0.39
12	340.20	12	0.42
13	368.55	13	0.46
14	396.90	14	0.49
15	425.25	15	0.53
16	453.60	16	0.57

Pounds	Kilograms	Kilograms	Pounds
1	0.454	1	2.205
2	0.91	2	4.41
3	1.36	3	6.61
4	1.81	4	8.82
5	2.27	5	11.02
6	2.72	6	13.23
7	3.18	7	15.43
8	3.63	8	17.64
9	4.08	9	19.84
10	4.54	10	22.05
11	4.99	11	24.26
12	5.44	12	26.46
13	5.90	13	28.67
14	6.35	14	30.87
15	6.81	15	33.08

Equivalent Measures

pinch or dash .... less than 1/8 teaspoon
2 teaspoons equals .... 1 tablespoon
4 tablespoon equals .... 1/4 cup equals......2 ounces
5 tablespoons plus 1 teaspoon equals............ 1/3 cup
8 tablespoons equals ...... 1/2 cup equals......4 ounces
16 tablespoons equals .....1 cup equals........8 ounces
2 cups equals ....1 pint
2 pints equals .... 1 quart
4 quarts equals .... 1 gallon
16 ounces equals .... 1 pound (dry measure)
1 stick butter equals .... 1/2 cup equals........4 ounces
1 cup cream equals ....2 cups whipped cream
1 pound cheese equals .... 4 cups grated cheese
1 medium onion equals ....1/2 cup chopped
1 medium orange equals .... 1/3 cup juice
1 medium orange rind equals .... 1 tablespoon grated
1 medium lemon equals.............. 3 tablespoons juice
1 medium lemon rind equals .... 2 teaspoons grated
1 cup quick-cooking rice equals...........2 cups cooked
1 cup long grain rice equals ....4 cups cooked
1 cup converted rice equals .... 3 cups cooked
1 pound brown or granulated sugar equals ....2 cups
1 pound confectionery sugar equals ....4 cups
1 pound sifted all-purpose flour equals ....4 cups

TABLE OF CONTENTS

INDEX

14

INDEX (Continued)

ALPHABETICAL INDEX

ALPHABETICAL INDEX (Continued)

This is a great dip for a party!

Avocado Dip

3 to 5 avocados, mashed
juice of ½ of a lemon
½ teaspoon salt
1 can green chile salsa
1 medium red onion, finely chopped
1 small can of black olives, chopped
2 medium tomatoes, peeled and chopped
½ lb. shredded cheddar cheese
½ lb. shredded jack cheese
corn or tortilla chips

Layer the ingredients in a deep dish. I usually start with the cheeses, then the salsa, onions, olives, tomatoes, and last the mashed avocados.

Baby Bay Shrimp Dip

1 lb. baby bay shrimp, washed in lemon water
½ cup mayonnaise
Dijon mustard to taste

Mix mayonnaise with mustard to taste. Place sauce in a small, deep bowl in the middle of plate. Arrange shrimp around the sauce. Place some toothpicks there for easy handling of the shrimp. Garnish with fresh parsley sprigs or watercress.

The day we broke ground for our new home, my darling next door neighbor, Diane Yardley (wife of George Yardley of great basketball fame), was thoughtful enough to prepare this delicious dip for us. It is elegant and just great!

Caviar Mold

8 hard boiled eggs
½ onion, very finely chopped
½ cup mayonnaise
  salt to taste
  white pepper to taste
  about 2 ounces of sour cream
  about 3 ounces of caviar

Chop the eggs and mix with the onion and mayonnaise. Salt and pepper to taste. Shape mixture into a mound and spread a thin layer of sour cream over entire mixture; then cover with a layer of caviar.

To decorate, cut cucumber rounds and place them all around the dip.

This mold also goes nicely with crackers or very thin bread which has been toasted.

Here's a zesty little appetizer that's sure to please. You can also serve this after your entree, in a salad plate with Bibb lettuce and the dressing of your choice. Two thin slices of Fried Camembert with maybe a small tomato rose or a slice of tomato will add color. But be sure to keep your salad small because the Camembert, though delicious and different, is filling and you still need room for the dessert.

Fried Camembert

6 wedges Camembert cheese
½ cup flour
½ cup bread crumbs
1 egg
2 tablespoons milk
  peanut oil

In a shallow mixing bowl, beat egg and milk and set aside.

Dip wedges of cheese quickly into ice water; dredge through flour. Dip cheese wedges in egg and milk mixture and roll them in bread crumbs until thoroughly coated. Refrigerate 10-15 minutes.

In a skillet, heat oil until very hot. Saute cheese wedges until crust turns a golden brown. Serve hot.

A fabulous hors d'oeuvre.

Greek Spinach Triangles
(Espino Copitas)

1 package Filo dough
10 ounces frozen chopped spinach
8 ounces feta cheese, crumbled
2 eggs
  white pepper
2 tablespoons unsalted butter
2 tablespoons finely chopped onions
1 clove garlic or ½ teaspoon "ready to use" garlic
1 tablespoon dill

Cut the Filo dough into three-inch strips. Separate into single layers.

Mix together the remaining ingredients. Drop a heaping tea-spoonful of the spinach mixture in one of the corners of a strip. Fold the corner over so that the end of the strip is now a diagonal line. Continue folding in this manner until the strip ends. Place the folded filo doughs upon a greased cookie sheet. Brush the triangles with melted butter. Bake in a 350° oven for 15 minutes, or until golden brown.

Simply delicious, everybody's favorite!

Mushroom Caps Appetizer

20 small size mushrooms
 4 tablespoons chopped chives
 4 tablespoons butter
 ¼ teaspoon thyme
 ¼ teaspoon basil
 ¼ teaspoon sage
 ¾ cup dry vermouth
   salt and pepper to taste

Over medium heat, melt butter in skillet. When hot, but not brown, add mushroom caps. tops down. Cook until golden. Then turn over and proceed in the same manner. Once golden on each side, add herbs, salt and pepper, vermouth, and increase heat to permit alcohol to evaporate. Add chives after liquid is reduced to half. Cook another minute, or until liquid is almost gone. Serve on dish of your choice with toothpicks.

*I am sure you will love this canape and fix it often.
It is so good.*

Onion Canapes

> 6 slices very thinly sliced white bread
> 1 medium-size onion, finely chopped
> ½ cup mayonnaise

Trim crust from all 4 sides of bread to make a neat square. Cut the bread into fourths; either into squares, triangles, or rounds. Butter the bread.

Mix together the mayonnaise and the onion. Spoon the onion mixture on top (on the heaping side) of bread and broil until slightly golden. I keep the door to the oven opened to avoid burning.

This is a very well liked canape.

Here is another of those simple recipes. It is so delicious, I had to include it.

Prune Canape

> prunes, pitted
> walnuts
> lean bacon strips

Preheat oven to 425°. Put a large piece of walnut inside prune. Wrap it with a raw piece of bacon, using a toothpick to hold together. Arrange on a baking sheet and bake until bacon is crisp. Drain on paper towels. Serve warm.

Artichokes are good for you and contain only 53 calories. With this combination of herbs you don't need any dressing, but that's up to your own taste.

Steamed Artichokes

With kitchen shears, cut pointed top from leaves of the artichoke. Cut off stem. Spread leaves slightly. Place artichokes, upright, on a steaming rack and place into a deep pot. Season to taste with onion powder, garlic powder, parsley, salt and white pepper. Add just enough water to touch bottom of artichokes. Steam for an hour or until tender. If necessary, keep adding more water.

Classic dip!

Guacamole

3 ripe avocados, peeled, seeded and mashed
2 large tomatoes, peeled and chopped
¼ cup onion, finely chopped
2 tablespoons lemon juice
½ cup green chile, diced
   tabasco sauce to taste (optional)
   garlic salt and white pepper to taste

Mix all ingredients together. This is traditionally served with tortilla chips. However, guacamole is delicious with any kind of chip or cracker.

Note:
To peel a tomato, spear a fork into the stem-end and plunge it into boiling hot water for a few seconds. Let cool a bit and peel carefully with a sharp knife.

Your guests won't forget you for having served this great appetizer.

Petite Crepes and Smoked Salmon

Use basic crepe batter. Make crepes about 3 inches in diameter and about ¼ inch thick. Use 2 crepes for each plate. Top with a slice of smoked salmon, a dollop of sour cream, your choice of caviar and some fresh dill.

Divine!

Salmon Canapes

Cut thinly sliced white bread into rounds, 1½" in diameter. Spread them with soft butter or margarine.

Chop finely two hard-boiled eggs. Mix with some finely chopped white onions and enough mayonnaise to hold the mixture together. Spread a thick layer over bread rounds and top with a slice of smoked salmon.

Low calorie appetizer — just great!

Stuffed Cucumber

1 large cucumber
1 cup flaked tuna fish
2 tablespoons mayonnaise
2 grated onions
½ teaspoon lemon juice
   dash of Worcestershire sauce
   dash of salt
   dash of paprika

Pare, and trim ends of cucumber. Remove the center of the cucumber with a zucchini corer.

Combine the remaining ingredients. Fill cucumber very tight. Chill thoroughly. Slice cross-wise into ½ inch slices. Serve cold.

Terry's Hors d'oeuvre Doll

One of the most beautiful persons I met at the restaurant is Terry Spreen, my darling friend from Costa Rica. Terry is a real beauty and can put any glamour girl to shame. She has an unbelieveable artistic ability and just seeing her occasionally inspires me.

Terry taught me the most facinating way to serve hors d' oeuvres (photo on page 36). Try it and you will see what I mean. Your guests will rave for hours.

The umbrella is made with watermelon rind and fresh flowers. The ribbon around her waist is made with cucumber.

Beautiful things fascinate me, so I must tell you about this most perfect evening at the restaurant. I still think about it, even though it took place over a year ago. Jacque, (a stunning red-head with cat eyes), and her husband, Dr. Robert Heebner, took over the restaurant for a private party, honoring, to me, two of the most talented individuals in the whole world, Gary Schott and Rob Friedline. Their talent for flower arranging is not to be believed. It is breath-taking. Their company, Floral Decor, turned the restaurant into an enchanted paradise. The floral arrangements had every specie of flower. From torch ginger, flown in from Hawaii, to the most exotic of orchids. All of this mixed with tree branches, ribbons, birds, and millions of little candles, all reflecting in the mirrors and crystals. The menu was super, supervised by Jacque. I will give the recipes later.

Now . . . if it is possible to gild the lily, we did with the incredible talent of concert violinist, Shony Alex Braun, who played steadily for hours to the delight of everyone. Truly an evening to remember.

Le Menu

SHRIMP COCKTAIL
Peruvian Style

CONSOMME AU SHERRY

FILET MIGNON AUX CHAMPIGNONS

SALADE POMMEE

FROMAGE — BRIE

CREPE WITH MOUSSE DE CHOCOLAT

CORDIALS

Most exotic! Always make salad dressing two days before you intend to use it, to allow flavors to blend.

Belgian Endive Salad

Serves 4

4 heads Belgian endive
4 ounces blue cheese, crumbled
1½ cups vinaigrette salad dressing

Put endive in a strainer and run very hot water from tap, this gets all the bitterness out, then sprinkle lemon juice over them to keep them from turning brown.

Dry with paper towels. Sprinkle crumbled blue cheese on top. Pour dressing over and serve.

Vinaigrette.
Combine the following ingredients:

1 cup olive oil
½ cup wine vinegar
2 garlic cloves, pressed (optional)
1 teaspoon salt
½ teaspoon pepper, freshly ground
½ teaspoon dry mustard

This is an elegant luncheon entree. You can also serve this as an appetizer for dinner if you cut the papayas into wedges and top with shrimp and mayonnaise sauce. Serve with lemon wedge.

Papaya Stuffed with Curried Bay Shrimp

Serves 4

2 papayas (½ papaya per person)
2 lbs. bay shrimp, cooked and cleaned
½ cup mayonnaise
1 teaspoon curry powder
salt and white pepper to taste

Cut the papayas in half. Peel, seed, and cut a small piece from the back of each half so that papaya sits well on plate. Refrigerate.

Mix mayonnaise, curry powder, salt and white pepper to taste. Wash shrimp in lemon water and drain well. Mix shrimp with mayonnaise mixture. Stuff into papaya halves. Garnish with fruits or lettuce and lemon slices.

Crab Cucumber Mousse

3 cups crab meat, picked-over and flaked
2 envelopes gelatin, unflavored
4½ tablespoons lemon juice
2 tablespoons sherry
2 teaspoons mustard
1½ cups mayonnaise
   white pepper
1 cup minced celery
1½ cups minced cucumber
4 tablespoons pimiento
3 drops green food coloring

Dissolve the gelatin in lemon juice and sherry over hot water. Use a large double-boiler or a metal bowl set over a saucepan of hot water. Stir in all other ingredients and mix well. Pour into an oiled 6-cup ring mold. Refrigerate for at least 4 hours or until set. Unmold onto a serving dish. Garnish with lettuce and carrot curls.

Caviar is an acquired taste, but I liked it from the very start. Duke had a passion for good caviar. When he was filming "Legend of The Lost" with Sophia Loren in Rome, she taught him to put a big scoop of caviar on a baked potato with some sour cream. That was always a treat to him. But the first time I ever had it was when we were staying in London for the

filming of "Circus World," and one evening Dimitri Tiomkin, the world famous composer, asked us out to dinner. He took us to this most elegant restaurant where we were escorted to probably the best table in the room. Dimitri turned to the maitre d' and said "bring my favorite for the three of us." I could not believe my eyes when a few minutes later there came this huge ice camel, and from one pack bag hangs a bottle of ice cold Stolichnaya Vodka, and from the other about five pounds of caviar! There must have been five waiters around our table serving this delicacy. There were blinis and chopped onions, chopped eggs, sour cream, wedges of lemon wrapped in yellow tulle. It was scrumptious. Dimitri lifted his ice cold Stolichnaya and said "Skoll." I almost fell out of my seat. The Vodka was so strong, but very smooth. Since then this has been my favorite way to start a super sit down dinner!

Caviar Crepes

Serves 4

8 prepared crepes, about 4-inch diameter
3 ounces caviar
4 eggs, hard-boiled and coarsely chopped
1 small onion, finely chopped
1 pint sour cream

Mix eggs with onions, a little caviar, and enough sour cream to hold together. Place 2 tablespoons of this mixture on a crepe and roll. Place on a small plate with seams down. On top of crepe, put more caviar. Decorate plate with lemon wedges.

Serve with iced-cold Vodka. (Keep your Vodka in the freezer.)

CAVIAR CREPES

CRAB CUCUMBER MOUSSE

PERUVIAN CAUSA

TERRY'S HORS D'OEUVRES DOLL

When we first got married, we lived in Encino, and Hampton J. Scott (affectionately called Scotty) was Duke's right-hand man. Besides taking care of every little detail around the house, he also happened to be an excellent chef. This is one of his salads that we liked very much.

Cottage Cheese Salad

      cottage cheese
      lettuce
      cheddar cheese, grated
      pineapple rings
      maraschino cherry

On a salad plate, arrange a bed of lettuce. Top with a big scoop of cottage cheese. Place a pineapple ring on top of the cottage cheese; cover with grated cheddar cheese. And to garnish, add a maraschino cherry on top. The combination of cheeses and pineapple is delicious.

Papaya and Grapefruit Salad

Serves 4

    1 head Boston lettuce
    1 papaya, peeled, seeded and sliced
        lengthwise into slices
    1 grapefruit, peeled, sectioned, and
        membranes removed
    1 purple onion, finely sliced
    1 cup Poppy Seed Dressing (page 38)

Onto chilled salad plates, (I put mine into the freezer for a while) arrange some lettuce leaves. Then, arrange the papaya, grapefruit, onion, and pour on the dressing.

Poppy Seed Dressing

Makes 3½ cups

3/4 cup sugar
2 teaspoons dry mustard
2 teaspoons salt
2/3 cup white vinegar
3 tablespoons onions, chopped very fine
1-1/2 cups salad oil
3 tablespoons poppy seeds

Mix sugar, mustard, salt and vinegar. Add onions and stir thoroughly. Add oil slowly, beating constantly with a whisk, until mixture thickens somewhat. Add poppy seeds and beat an additional minute.

Store in a cool place or in the refrigerator. Stir well before using.

A terrific appetizer and very low calorie.

Broiled Grapefruit

Cut grapefruit in half and remove membrane. Add brown sugar and cinnamon.

Put under broiler until bubbly hot.

This is just superb for a buffet, and it is beautiful to look at.

Guacamole Mousse

1 cup cold water
1½ tablespoons unflavored gelatin
1 cup boiling water
3 cups coarsely chopped avocado
1 tablespoon lemon juice
1 tablespoon Worcestershire sauce
2 teaspoons salt
    dash of tabasco
¾ cup whipping cream, whipped
¾ cup mayonnaise
2 hard-boiled eggs, chopped
1 tomato, peeled and chopped

In the cold water, soak gelatin; then add the boiling water. Add avocado, lemon juice, Worcestershire sauce, salt and tabasco. Chill until mixture is almost set.

Fold whipped cream into mayonnaise. Add the avocado mixture. Oil a 4-cup mold lightly, and pour in the mixture. Chill until very well set. Garnish with chopped eggs and tomato, after turning-out onto a serving dish.

Probably one of the most fabulous restaurants in Orange County is the Villa Fontana. The food is consistently divine. Years ago, because of our mutual interest in tennis, I was fortunate to meet the owners, Ariane and Henry Grum, and I have treasured our friendship ever since. We have been practically all over the world playing in tennis tournaments, and have enjoyed great times together.

Probably the best parties I've ever attended have been the private parties given by the Grums at the Villa. People have been known to fly in from all over the world in their private jets, when they are lucky enough to receive that oh so precious invitation.

Henry gave me three recipes from his private collection that I am sure you will enjoy!

Mimosa Salad "Villa Fontana"

Serves 4

2 heads Bibb lettuce
4 hard-boiled eggs, chopped
2 ripe tomatoes, chopped
4 tablespoons finely cut chives

Cut 2 heads of Bibb lettuce into 8 wedges. Wash carefully, dry, and place 2 wedges on each plate. Cover with hard-boiled choped eggs, tomatoes, and finely cut chives. Cover with dressing.

Dressing:
1/3 cup red wine vinegar
2/3 cup olive oil
1/2 medium white onion, minced
1 tablespoon sliced pimiento

40

1½ teaspoon salt
1 tablespoon Dijon mustard
¼ teaspoon white pepper
1 garlic clove, pressed
dash of tabasco

Mix all ingredients and place in covered container in refrigerator for at least 2 hours. This dressing will keep a whole month in refrigerator.

Lime Mold

1 6-ounce package lime gelatin
2 cups boiling water
2 cups sour cream
1 17-ounce can crushed pineapple, undrained
½ cup chopped walnuts

In a mixing bowl, dissolve gelatin in boiling water. Add sour cream and whip with rotary beater. Fold in pineapple and walnuts.

Pour into an 8-cup mold, and chill until well set.

Here is an easy way to unmold this recipe. Carefully run the point of a knife around the inside edge of mold. Place serving plate over mold opening and invert. Place a hot towel on top of the mold and let stand until mold can be easily lifted.

Even if you don't like tomatoes, you will love this salad! The first time we ever had it was in the south of France. Our hostess, Florence Garrett, served it with a Sole Mousse, stuffed with Lobster Newburg. (This recipe is also in this book.) I love her for giving me both recipes and they have been served in my home whenever I want to "fish" for compliments.

Salade de Tomates Cote D' Azur

4 medium size ripe, but firm, tomatoes
1 medium size red onion, chopped coarsely
2 tablespoons finely chopped parsley
3 tablespoons olive oil
2 tablespoons red wine vinegar
2 tablespoons Herbes de Provence*
    salt and pepper to taste

Slice tomatoes ¼ inch thick, and arrange them on a pretty platter or on individual chilled salad plates (3 slices per plate). Sprinkle onions on top, then spoon on oil, then vinegar, salt and pepper. Finally, sprinkle tomatoes generously with the Herbes de Provence and parsley.

*Herbes de Provence mixture consists of ⅛ teaspoon each of crushed basil, thyme, oregano and rosemary.

I grew up with Seviche, so I love it. You can also use other kinds of fish, including shrimp or lobster. I prepare this dish quite often when I am trying to get rid of a few pounds.

My children also like Seviche very much, so it is always a regular in our home.

Seviche

1½ lbs. scallops
   juice of 12 lemons
   juice of 2 limes
½ large white onion
2 ripe tomatoes
½ chopped green bell pepper
1 small can of chopped chiles
8 green olives, pitted
1 bunch cilantro
1 teaspoon sugar
   garlic salt to taste

Cut scallops into bite-size pieces and put them in a strainer. Pour boiling water over scallops. Submerge scallops in lemon and lime juice. Slice onion very thinly; chop tomatoes into small pieces; chop green olives, and add to scallop mixture. Add chopped chiles and season with salt, pepper, garlic salt, and sugar to taste. Add finely chopped cilantro, discarding the stems. Marinate Seviche for at least 12 hours or overnight. Serve chilled. Seviche will keep nicely in refrigerator for four days.

I guess we never forget certain things about our childhood, specially Mother's cooking. When I first came to California and made it my home, I struggled with a lot of foods I could not imagine anyone eating, like something as icky-sweet as fudge or divinity or cheese cake or even apple pie. Over the years my taste has changed and I do eat apple pie now and love it, but I still dislike terribly sweet things.

We also have a lot of dishes in Peru like we have here, but they vary slightly, like our shrimp cocktail. I find it divine but then I like the combination of the avocado with the shrimp. Try it for a really exotic look.

Shrimp Cocktail Peruvian Style

Serves 6

    catsup
    mayonnaise
1 head iceberg lettuce, finely shredded
2 avocados, peeled, seeded, and sliced
1 lb. bay shrimp, cooked and chilled,
     with a few drops of lemon juice
2 hard-boiled eggs, sliced
1 ripe tomato, sliced (optional)

Mix catsup and mayonnaise until coral in color. This is your sauce.

In a shrimp cocktail dish or a tall stemmed glass, like a champagne glass, place shredded lettuce. On top, place sliced avocados. Place shrimp on top of this and cover with sauce. Garnish with slices of hard-boiled eggs and tomato slices.

Once again I am between chefs. So I look for my chef's hat and off to the kitchen I go. I check the menu for the evening and to my horror the salad to be served is spinach salad. Well, I had not the vaguest idea of how to prepare one. My friend, Joan Stemm came to mind. Just the week before I had dinner at her home and she served spinach salad, the best I've ever had. I am still grateful that she was home that evening and was willing to share her recipe.

Spinach Salad

Serves 6

2 bunches fresh spinach,
    washed and stems discarded
½ cup vegetable oil
¼ cup red wine vinegar
1 tablespoon powdered sugar
6 mushrooms, sliced
2 hard-boiled eggs, grated
6 strips of bacon, crisp, drained and crumbled

In a saucepan heat the oil, vinegar and sugar. Pour over clean spinach and mix. Add the mushrooms, eggs, and bacon.

Julienne Carrot Salad

Serves 4

4 carrots
½ cup canned tangerines, save juice
½ cup chopped walnuts
¼ cup raisins

Julienne the carrots. Mix with tangerines and just a touch of the juice. Add the walnuts and the raisins.

I was filming my second motion picture in probably the most beautiful benign jungle on the Amazon River in a town called Tingo Maria. One morning the company was gathered together having breakfast and reading the morning papers when someone casually said, "John Wayne just arrived in Lima and is searching for locations to film a movie."

I have never been much of a movie goer, but I knew the name John Wayne, yet in my mind I could not quite place him. It used to take a movie ten years after it was released to play in Lima, Peru. I thought of Gary Cooper and Randolph Scott or some movie I could possibly identify him with. Anyway, we went to work and I dismissed the whole conversation from my mind.

We were deep into a scene, after the director said "cut, lunch time", he took me aside and said "John Wayne has hired a private plane and is coming over, he wants to meet a Peruvian movie company at work".

Our producer said everyone could have the rest of the afternoon off, so back we went to our beautiful hotel right at the edge of the Amazon.

As I walked into the hotel a friend of mine said "Pilar come here, I want you to meet John Wayne." I looked up to what seemed to me the tallest, most handsome man I have ever met.

The company decided to give a small dinner party in his honor and I was seated next to John Wayne. At first I was apprehensive, I had never met a big movie star and did not know what to expect. His very close friend Ernie Saftig was traveling with him, and they were enjoying every bit of their first trip to South America.

We started to make some conversation and I said something to him I could have cut my tongue for, I said "You were wonderful in 'For Whom The Bells Toll'." Suddenly there was complete silence at the table, after what seemed like an eternity Duke and Ernie started laughing hysterically and Duke very nicely said, "You are thinking of Gary Cooper; have you seen 'The Quiet Man'?" I said, "I had not only not seen it, I never heard of it." He said, "Do you ever go to the movies?" I replied, "very rarely." Duke said, "Try to see it, you will like it."

The rest of the evening was fun. He told me that Ernie and he would be flying back to Lima first thing in the morning on their way to Santiago, Chile.

I had to get up at 5:00 a.m. for the next day's shooting so I excused myself, never thinking that sixty days later, and 4,000 miles away we would be dining together again.

Heart of Palm or Palmito grows abundantly in Tingo Maria. During this particular location we must have had Heart of Palm salad with every meal. Here is one of my favorite ways to serve it.

Tingo Maria
Heart of Palm Salad

Makes approx. 1 cup

¾ cup salad oil
6 tablespoons fresh lemon juice
1 teaspoon salt
1 teaspoon sugar
½ teaspoon paprika

47

¾ teaspoon aromatic bitters (Angostura)
2 tablespoons finely minced celery
4 tablespoons finely minced pimiento-stuffed green olives
4 tablespoons finely minced scallions with tops
Hearts of Palm

Mix all ingredients together except Hearts of Palm. Spoon a tablespoon or two on each serving of bibb lettuce arranged with Hearts of Palm. Garnish with sliced pimientos, chopped walnuts and diced apples.

Quick, easy, and oooh so good, this is almost a meal in itself. It's just great for a bridge luncheon, I usually serve it with monkey bread.

Summer Salad

Serves 4

1 head of lettuce, leaf or Boston
1 can asparagus, drained and cut in bite sizes
1 can celery, drained and cut in bite sizes
1 can of tuna, 15 ounces
4 hard-boiled eggs
salt and pepper to taste
Italian dressing

Tear lettuce into bite-sized pieces and place in a large salad bowl. Add asparagus and celery. Drain tuna and flake over vegetables. Toss lightly. Cut 2 hard-boiled eggs into wedges and add to salad. Finely chop the 2 remaining eggs and set aside. Season with salt and freshly ground pepper to taste.

Drizzle dressing over salad and toss lightly. Top with chopped hard-boiled eggs. Serve on chilled salad plates.

Divine and simple summer entree.

Tomatoes Stuffed with Egg Salad

Serves 4

    4 tomatoes, one per person
    4 eggs, hard-boiled and chopped
    6 tablespoons celery, chopped
    4 tablespoons mayonnaise

Cut upper part of the tomato and remove the pulp, turn upside down to drain on paper towels.

In a deep narrow bowl mix the other ingredients and stuff the tomato with the egg mixture. Serve on chilled salad plates and garnish with Bibb lettuce. Sprinkle paprika over the egg salad so it will look real pretty.

You can also use this basic recipe and exchange the eggs for tuna.

Guacamole Salad

    Bibb lettuce
    tomatoes, peeled, sliced thickly
    guacamole (page 25)
    hard-boiled eggs, chopped

Arrange lettuce and top with tomato slices. Finish by topping with guacamole and eggs.

A divine soup anytime and anyplace.

Artichoke Soup

Serves 6

¼ cup vegetable oil
4 tablespoons finely chopped shallots
 freshly ground white pepper to taste
4 tablespoons flour
3 cups chicken broth
17 ounces canned artichoke bottoms,
 drained, sliced
1 teaspoon fresh lemon juice
½ cup heavy cream
1 teaspoon lemon zest
2 tablespoons finely chopped fresh parsley

In a saucepan, heat oil using low heat. Add shallots and pepper; cook for a couple of minutes, then stir in flour. Over medium-high heat add broth and bring to a boil, stirring constantly. Add artichokes and lemon juice. Reduce heat and simmer for 30 minutes. Cool and process through a blender.

Just before serving, stir in cream and lemon zest. Garnish with a dollop of sour cream and chopped parsley.

Note:
Should you want to make this soup as an *Artichoke Vichyssoise,* proceed in the same manner as above; refrigerate until very cold and serve.

This soup became a favorite at the restaurant and you will see why, it is absolutely delicious.

Asparagus Bisque

4 cups fresh or frozen asparagus
2 cups chopped celery
7 cups chicken broth
6 tablespoons butter or margarine
1 cup heavy cream or half and half
  salt and pepper to taste
  a dash of nutmeg

Place asparagus and celery in boiling water. Boil for five minutes. Add salt. Drain excess liquid. Place in blender and add little by little the chicken broth. Blend until smooth. Melt butter and add the salt, white pepper and nutmeg. Mix together with the chicken broth. Stir in vegetables, add the cream and serve.

We have a delightful custom in Lima, everytime you give a party, large or small, you greet your guests at the door with a very small cup of either chicken or beef broth. The purpose of this makes very good sense, the broth will coat and warm your stomach and prepare it for the cocktails you are about to drink or the food you are going to consume. I have done this a couple of times at our home and my guests have just loved it. So, here are the recipes.

Chicken Broth

6 chicken breasts or other cuts (no skin)
4 carrots
6 stalks celery
1 bell pepper, chopped
1 bunch cilantro
2 bay leaves
4 peppercorns
2 cubes chicken stock
1 white onion with 3 cloves encrusted
2 turnips, medium size
1 large leek, well washed
(section the green part of the leek
so it washes better)

Remove skin from chicken, put into a pot, cover with water and add rest of ingredients. Bring to a boil then simmer for at least two hours. Cool. Remove chicken and save for chicken salad or whatever.

Strain the broth by passing through cheese cloth, discard vegetables, freeze overnight. The fat will rise to the top and will be easy to remove. You will have a delicious clear broth.

Different Ways To Use This Broth:

1. To greet your guests with a demi-tasse when they arrive at your home.

2. To start an elegant sit down dinner.

3. For dieting — sipped through the day with a few drops of lemon. (if desired)

4. To cook vegetables in, when on a fat free diet.

Simply marvelous!

Soupe de Tomates a la Provencale

Serves 6

    1 onion
    2 leeks
    4 tablespoons olive oil
    4 cups tomatoes, canned
    6 cups chicken broth
    ½ teaspoon fennel seed
    2 teaspoons thyme
    2 bay leaves
    2 teaspoons basil
      grated peel of 1 orange

In a large saucepan or kettle, heat the oil and saute onions and leeks. Add the rest of the ingredients and simmer for 30 minutes.

Chicken and Dumplings Soup

Serves 6

> 1 3-lb. chicken or equivalent parts
> 1 medium onion, quartered
> 6 black peppercorns
> 1 celery rib, cut into 1" pieces
> 1 carrot, cut into 1" pieces
> 2 sprigs parsley
> 1 teaspoon salt

In an 8-quart pot, place all ingredients. Add cold water to cover by about 2 inches. Heat to a boil; then reduce heat to a simmer. Cook until chicken is tender, about 45 minutes. Remove the chicken to a dish.

Strain the broth into a clean pot. Discard vegetables. Remove chicken meat from bones and cut meat into bite-size pieces. Add meat to soup. Heat until hot. Prepare dumplings and proceed to add them to chicken soup.

Dumplings:
> 1 egg
> 1/3 cup milk
> 1 cup flour
> 1/4 teaspoon salt
> 1 teaspoon baking powder

In a bowl, beat the egg with a wire whisk. Add milk, flour, salt and baking powder, and stir well. Batter should be medium-thick. Drop small spoonfuls into simmering, near boiling, soup. When all the dumplings have been added, cover pot and simmer for 15 minutes. Serve hot.

Cream of Carrot Soup

    1 lb. carrots
    1 lb. potatoes
    2 tablespoons butter
    ½ cup coarsely chopped onion
    6 cups chicken broth
    2 sprigs fresh thyme or ½ teaspoon dried
    1 bay leaf
    1 cup cream
      tabasco (just a little)
    ½ teaspoon Worcestershire sauce
    ½ teaspoon sugar
      salt and pepper to taste
    1 cup cold milk

Peel carrots and potatoes. Cut carrots into rounds and cube potatoes. Melt butter in a pot and add onion. Add the carrots, potatoes and chicken and bring to a boil. Add thyme and bay leaf. Reduce heat and simmer 30 to 40 minutes until carrots and potatoes are tender.

Puree in a food processor or blender until smooth.

Return to pot; add remaining ingredients and heat thoroughly. Serve hot.

This is a must!

Corn Chowder

Serves 6

4 tablespoons butter
1 white onion, chopped
4 cups chicken broth
1 large potato, chopped
4 cups corn, fresh cooked or canned
½ teaspoon thyme
1 bay leaf
1 cup cream, half and half
6 tablespoons butter

Saute onions in the 4 tablespoons butter until they are tender and translucent. Add the corn, potatoes, chicken broth and herbs. Simmer for 25 minutes. Puree the soup in a blender. Return to pot. Before serving add the cream, butter, and check the seasoning. Serve hot.

This is the original Soupe a l'oignon served at "Les Halles" in Paris, France.

French Onion Soup

Serves 6

4 large onions, finely chopped
6 tablespoons bacon fat drippings
2 tablespoons flour
2 cloves garlic, mashed
   salt and pepper to taste
1 quart chicken stock
1 cup dry white wine
1 sprig of parsley
¼ teaspoon thyme
1 tablespoon Cognac
½ teaspoon "Kitchen Bouquet" (browning agent)
1 loaf French bread
   Parmesan cheese

In a deep saucepan heat bacon drippings, then saute the onions and cook over medium heat until onions are just soft. Add flour, salt, pepper and garlic; stir and cook until mixture is golden brown, but not burned.

Add parsley, thyme, chicken stock and dry white wine; simmer for 45 minutes. Add cognac. Add ½ teaspoon Kitchen Bouquet.

Serve in individual ovenproof bowls with a slice (half an inch thick) of roasted French bread in each. Sprinkle with Parmesan cheese and a dot of butter; place under broiler until cheese melts and forms a brown crust.

Vichyssoise

Serves 6

4 leeks, only white part, sliced
1 medium onion, sliced
¼ cup butter
6 medium potatoes, peeled and sliced
1 quart chicken broth
2 tablespoons sherry, dry
1 tablespoon salt
2 cups milk
1 cup table cream
chopped chives

In a large pot saute leeks and onions in butter. Add potatoes, chicken broth, sherry and salt. Gently boil for 30 minutes. Potatoes should be very tender.

Press through a fine sieve or puree in an electric blender. This process will have to be done in portions until it is completed.

Return mixture to pot; add milk and 1 cup of the table cream. Bring to a boil and remove from heat. Let cool.

After cooling, put through a fine sieve. This time mixture must be put through a fine sieve to remove the vegetable pulp. Chill thoroughly.

Add remaining cream. Serve chilled and garnish with chopped chives.

Mushroom Bisque

Serves 6

6 tablespoons butter
½ cup finely chopped onion
6 tablespoons flour
6 cups chicken broth
½ cup finely ground walnuts
2 sprigs parsley
½ bay leaf
   pinch of thyme
   salt and white pepper to taste
¾ lb. mushrooms, stems and caps
   sliced separately
1 teaspoon lemon juice
   dash cayenne
2 egg yolks
½ cup heavy cream
1 tablespoon dry sherry

In a large saucepan, melt 4 tablespoons butter and saute onion until soft. Add and stir in the flour, using medium heat, and cook for a few minutes. Add chicken broth and blend. Add parsley, bay leaf, thyme and mushroom stems. Reduce heat and simmer, covered, for about 15 minutes.

Melt 2 tablespoons butter in a skillet and saute sliced mushroom caps. Season with salt, pepper and lemon juice. Set aside.

Strain broth into a bowl, pressing mushroom stems to extract juice. Return broth to saucepan, and add mushroom caps, sherry and Cayenne pepper. Continue to simmer.

In a bowl, beat egg yolks and cream, and gradually add to soup, stirring while adding. Heat well, but do not let it boil. Serve hot.

A precious friend of mine is Coy Mirkin. Talk about ups and downs . . . our lives have been like a see-saw. But, the nice thing is that there has always been laughter through it all. She is not only beautiful to look at, but also a great cook; except you can never pin her down to a recipe. It's, "a dash of this, or two shakes of that and some oregano." When you ask, "How much oregano?" she looks you straight in the eye and says, "I don't know. How much do you think?" So then you give up and ask, "Well, how about that other dish you served last week?"

I guess I'm lucky. I managed to get this recipe from her and it is just great!

Acapulco Casserole

Serves 4

1 medium-size can chili (no beans)
2 medium-size cans stewed tomatoes
3 cups corn chips
½ lb. cheddar cheese, shredded
1 cup black olives, pitted, sliced
  chiles, optional

Preheat oven to 350°.

In a casserole, layer the chile, tomatoes, cheese and corn chips. Top with the black olives and chiles if desired.

Bake for 30 minutes. Serve hot.

This recipe was given to me by Marge Wingfield from Nogales, Arizona. One weekend the whole family was invited to their ranch and a wonderful time we all had. While the children went horseback riding, Marge and I would play tennis all day long. Duke and Ralph Wingfield literally spent the whole weekend playing and arguing gin-rummy. In the evenings we always looked forward to very special meals under Marge's supervision.

Baked Turbot

Serves 6

6 filets of fresh turbot
2 purple onions, medium size, thinly sliced
8 ounces sour cream
2 small cans of tomato sauce

Butter a 12" x 7" baking dish. Cover bottom with onions. Place fish filets on top of onions and sprinkle with a little salt and pepper. Cover with sour cream and top with tomato sauce. Bake at 350° for 1 hour.

My daughter Aissa is starting to show a great deal of interest in the culinary art. Here is one of her favorites — delicious!

Beef and Noodle Casserole

Serves 8

1½ lbs. lean ground beef
2 tablespoons butter
1 garlic clove, pressed
1 15-ounce can tomato sauce
1 teaspoon salt
1 teaspoon sugar
few grindings of black pepper
8 ounces dried egg noodles
6 green onions
1 cup sour cream
½ lb. cheddar cheese, shredded

In a skillet, brown beef in butter; add garlic, tomato sauce, salt, sugar and pepper. Reduce heat and simmer for 20 minutes.

Cook and drain the noodles. Chop the onions finely and mix with sour cream.

In a buttered casserole, arrange layers of the beef mixture, then a layer of noodles, then a thin layer of the sour cream mixture. End layering with the beef. Sprinkle cheese on top and bake for 20 minutes at 350°.

My childrens' favorite—

Beef Stew

One of the things that I love to cook is beef stew. Maybe it is because it is so easy, and is also a whole meal in one. And everybody loves it.

When I cook stew, I usually make it in the biggest pot I can find, as I make plenty of it. Then, I freeze it in small containers to use whenever. It's great for unexpected guests.

I start with stew meat and make sure that the fat is all cut off. Then I cut it into bite-size pieces. Then I add enough V-8 juice to cover the beef. Also, I add a snappy tomato flavoring which is rather hot. I find that these two juices mixed together give the meat an interesting flavor. Next, I add everything I can think of, like potatoes (peeled and cubed), corn, carrots, peas, string beans, red onions (chopped very small) and celery.

With this dish, you must use your imagination. For example, if you like a certain herb, you should add it to the stew. I happen to like a few drops of tabasco, but I tend to like my food on the spicy side.

Stew should be prepared one day before you are going to use it. It always tastes twice as good in the consecutive days.

Back to the recipe! Bring the juices and meat to a boil. Add vegetables. Immediately lower the heat and let it simmer for at least 2 hours.

Probably the most elegant buffet in town is at the Santa Anita Race Track, at the Turf Club. Under the careful supervision of Mr Tony Pope. Tony has been executive chef there for 28 years, his staff alone consists of 65 chefs.

I have had the pleasure of attending the lovely parties given there by Bobbie (Mrs. Robert Grant).

The display of food is something not to be believed. Their flower arrangements are made from fruits and vegetables. There are sail boats made out of potatoes, beautiful birds made out of apples (pictures on pages 106 and 107). I made friends with Tony and he was kind enough to give me a few of his recipes, for which I will give him credit. (pages 64-133-93)

Beef Stroganoff

2 lbs. beef tenderloin, cut in thin slivers
2 tablespoons flour
2 teaspoons freshly ground black pepper
1 teaspoon paprika
½ cup clarified butter
3 tablespoons shallots, finely chopped
2 tablespoons tomato paste
2 cups burgandy wine
1 cup brown sauce
1 lb. sauteed, sliced mushrooms
1 cup sour cream
2 tablespoons chopped parsley

Dredge the meat in the flour, mixed with the salt, pepper, and paprika. In a very hot skillet, saute the meat in the butter; very quickly. Keep on the rare side. Remove the meat, and keep warm. Add the shallots to the pan juices and cook briefly. Add the tomato paste, wine, and brown sauce. Bring to a boil, stirring until the sauce is thick. Add the mushrooms and the meat. Simmer for five minutes. Add some of the hot sauce to the sour cream, then stir the sour cream into the remaining sauce. Serve from a casserole sprinkled with parsley and more freshly ground black pepper.

Chicken a la Edie

Serves 6

1 per person - whole chicken breasts; divided, boned, skinned and pounded thin
1 per person - whole green chile with a slice of Jack
   cheese inside
   grated parmesan cheese
   eggs, beaten
   sweet butter
   Italian (Contadina) seasoned bread crumbs

Roll chile with slice of Jack cheese inside chicken breast. Secure with toothpick which can be taken out later.

Dip in beaten egg; then in seasoned bread crumbs and parmesan cheese. Refrigerate for at least 20 minutes.

Saute in sweet butter and brown lightly.

Place in casserole and bake at 350° for 35 minutes, uncovered.

Serve with salsa or mushroom sauce.

Chicken Tetrazzini

Serves 8

1/2 cup butter
8 mushrooms, sliced
1/3 cup flour
3-1/2 cups chicken broth
1 cup light cream
1/4 cup sherry, dry
1-1/2 teaspoons salt
1 cup grated Parmesan cheese
6 cups cooked chicken meat, diced
1 lb. thin spaghetti
2 tablespoons fresh, minced parsley

Break spaghetti strands into fourths. Start to prepare spaghetti, and have it nearly cooked before starting the sauce.

Preheat oven to 375°.

In a large saucepan, melt butter and saute mushrooms. Stir in flour and gradually add broth. Cook over medium heat until sauce is thickened. Add cream, sherry, salt and half of the cheese. Whisk and simmer for about 5 minutes.

Butter a large, round oven-ware dish. Make layers of spaghetti, chicken and the sauce, in order; ending with the sauce. Sprinkle with remainder of cheese.

Bake, uncovered, for about 35 minutes. Garnish with parsley and serve hot.

This is one of my sister Josephine's favorite recipes.

Chicken Breast with Beef

        8 chicken breasts, skinned and boned
          slices of dried beef
        1 can mushroom soup
        1 cup sour cream
        ¾ cup sherry
          salt and pepper to taste

Wrap each chicken breast with sliced dried beef and place seam side down in dish. Mix together mushroom soup, sour cream, sherry, salt and pepper. Pour mixture over chicken. Bake at 200° for 5 hours. You can prepare it the day before and cook it the next if so desired.

It is very easy and tasty — I serve it with wild rice and a canned peach or Jello molded salad.

Beef Wellington

Serves 6

        3 lbs. tenderloin of beef
        1 tablespoon vegetable oil
        1 lbs. mushrooms, minced
        2 tablespoons lemon juice
        5 tablespoons unsalted butter
        4 tablespoons chopped shallots
        1 tablespoons flour
        ½ cup Madeira wine

    salt and pepper to taste
½ teaspoon Herbes de Provence (page 42)
8 ounces Pate
1 lb. puff pastry
1 egg yolk
1 tablespoon milk

Preheat oven to 425°. Rub the meat with oil and place in a roasting pan. Place in upper third of oven and bake 30 minutes. Remove from oven, let cool, and refrigerate. Meat must be cold before wrapping in puff pastry.

Melt butter in a large frying pan; add mushrooms, lemon juice and shallots, saute them. Stir in flour until smooth; then add Madeira wine and boil until liquid is evaporated. Season and put through blender. Cool, then add the pate, mix well. Set aside.

Roll out pastry to ⅛ inch thick. Spread half the pate-mushroom mixture over the center of the pastry. Mix egg yolk and milk. Place meat on pastry and spread remainder of pate over it. Wrap the pastry around the cold tenderloin and seal carefully, using the egg mixture. Save any excess pieces of puff pastry and cut out decoration for the top of pastry jacket.

Seal with egg mixture. Pierce the pastry in a diagonal pattern and place the wrapped beef on a baking sheet and chill for at least 1 hour.

Insert a meat thermometer through the pastry into the thickest part of the meat. Paint the pastry with remainder of egg mixture. Bake in a 400° oven for about 30 minutes or until the meat thermometer reads 120°. Remove from oven and allow to cool at least 15 minutes. Cut into 1½ inch slices and serve.

BEEF WELLINGTON

MANICOTTI CREPES

70

GLAMOROUS MEAT LOAF

SCAMPI

Delicious over Cappelini noodles or rice.

Coral Scampi

Serves 6

    2 lbs. red shrimp (raw, shelled)
    4 cloves garlic, minced
    1 tablespoon dry oregano
    1 tablespoon chopped parsley
      salt and pepper to taste
    2 tablespoons cooking oil

Sauce:

    1 stick butter
    3 cloves garlic, minced
    2 tablespoons lemon juice
    2 tablespoons parsley, minced

Shell and butterfly raw shrimp. (butterfly by cutting down center of back. Do not cut completely through.) Spread open, tail up. In a shallow baking pan place oil and shrimp. Combine garlic, parsley, salt, pepper and oregano. Sprinkle over shrimp. Bake in 450° oven on **top** shelf for five minutes.

Sauce:

In frying pan, melt 1 stick butter, add 3 cloves pressed garlic, heat but do not brown as garlic will become bitter. Add lemon juice. Pour over shrimp and sprinkle with minced parsley.

Nancy Reagan is a gracious lady to have sent me these delicious recipes from the White House.

Cold Medallion of Lobster

with California Wine Salad Dressing

Allow three generous slices of lobster (whole medallion) per person.

Select greens with care, wash and store in plastic refrigerator bowl with a tea towel on the bottom to absorb water.

Chill salad plates and forks.

To serve, assemble by arranging lettuce curls on each plate, then heap on the shellfish.

Pour on the dressing and garnish with chopped chives and parsley.

California Wine Salad Dressing:

> 1/3 cup dry sherry
> 1/3 cup dry vermouth
>   1 cup dry white wine
>   1 cup best California olive oil
>   2 green onions, tops and all
> 1/2 teaspoon sugar
> 1/2 teaspoon dry mustard
> 1/2 teaspoon Beau Monde seasoning
> 1/2 teaspoon MSG seasoning
> 1/4 teaspoon salt
>   white pepper to taste
>   zest of lemon (grated rind of one lemon)

Run the green onions through an onion or garlic press into a mortar, add the dry ingredients. Then pour in your wines that have been mixed in a pyrex pitcher. After seasonings and wines have been well mixed, return to pyrex pitcher and slowly pour in olive oil, stirring constantly. Shake vigorously and taste to correct seasonings.

Note:

This salad dressing does not hold well and should be used within three or four days.

Elegant Flaming Beef

Serves 6

A filet of beef, if properly done, can be the most succulent meat in the world. Have your butcher cut your filet from the large end of the tenderloin. It should be about ten inches long and weigh nearly four pounds. It must be a good heavy filet. Cut as I describe, one will serve six.

Wipe well with a wet paper towel and pour a good Madeira over all. I use either Leacock Fine Dry Sercial Cocktail Madeira, or Rozes Fine Bual (medium dry) Madeira. Allow about a quarter of a cup for each piece of meat. Pepper well with Java cracked pepper and put into a cold oven and turn on to 300 degrees. Allow one and one-half hours cooking time basting four times at even intervals with the following sauce: The amounts given are for one four-pound tenderloin.

Cooking sauce for beef:

> 1/3 cube butter, melted
> 1/4 cup Madeira drippings from meat

Keep basting sauce hot, and take the beef out of the oven, pour pan drippings into the basting sauce and then baste meat copiously with sauce. Return to oven, and repeat process four times in all. All through the cooking period the thermostat is set at 300 degrees. If the beef is fat, you must skim off excess fat before each basting.

After the beef has been cooking for half an hour, or when brown, turn so the other side will brown. The Madeira has enough sweetness so the beef should be a lovely dark color.

I serve this meat so it looks like a real "production." My large silver tea tray is the basic holder. On top of it I put a silver sauce boat and a silver tray for the block of sliced pate. Cover the edges of the bigger tray with loads of parsley. Leave the center space empty to receive the meat platter. We use a large crepe pan so we can have it good and hot.

Have a cup of brandy warming on the stove. This will be the touch that contributes the glamour.

Remove the tenderloins from the oven. Then slice a portion off the large end so it will be level and you can stand these beauties upright. Place them carefully in the warmed crepe or serving platter. Then pour the sauce from the roasting pan over the meat and bring it to the serving table.

When the guests are assembled, pour the hot brandy over all the meat and flame. Keep spooning the brandy sauce over the beef until it is all burned out. The burning brandy merges all the flavors.

A tenderloin is the easiest thing in the world to carve but here is a tip: slice the meat in rather thin slices, for the pate and sauce would be lost on a great thick piece of beef. Each piece of beef will have medium, well done, and rare meat. The ends are more done than the center.

After carving put on each slice of beef a slice of pate and spoonful of sauce from the sauce boat (which is a different sauce from the cooking process.)

Serving sauce for the beef:

For one filet, serving 6

    1 can Campbell's beef bouillon
    2 teaspoons arrowroot, dissolved in some
      cold consomme
1 or 2 cans very large truffles, chopped
    8 mushroom stems, chopped
      (marinate truffles and mushrooms in Madeira)
 1/3 cup Madeira

Heat the soup, undiluted, saving some to dissolve the arrowroot in. Add slowly to the hot broth and cook on very low fire for about five minutes. Add the chopped truffles and mushrooms which have been marinating in the Madeira, pour the whole thing in, heat, and cook for a minute or two. This sauce can be made the day before and stored in a covered container in the refrigerator.

Serve bubbling hot, with a small sauce spoon over each slice of beef.

The 7½ ounce size of pate might be enough for 16 if you are an expert slicer. To be on the safe side, buy the 11 ounce block. Refrigerate and then slice carefully with a hot knife in the thinnest possible slices. Lay the slices on your serving dish and refrigerate, putting dish and all in a plastic bag. Whisk out when you are ready to serve your wondrous dish.

Cheese Souffle

½ cup butter (1 stick)
6 tablespoons flour
2 cups milk
2 cups grated cheddar cheese
1 teaspoon salt
1 teaspoon cayenne pepper
6 eggs, separated
¼ teaspoon cream of tartar
1 teaspoon Worcestershire sauce
grated parmesan cheese

Preheat oven to 400°.

In a saucepan, melt butter; add flour and whisk until well blended. Let cook for a few minutes over medium heat. Add milk and whisk until smooth. Cook until sauce thickens, maintaining medium heat. Add salt, cayenne pepper, Worcestershire sauce and cheddar cheese. After cheese has melted, remove from heat and let cool.

Whisk in the egg yolks and set aside. In a bowl, beat egg whites; when frothy add cream of tartar and continue beating until stiff peaks form. Add sauce to egg whites, very carefully, with a wooden spoon or rubber spatula. Fold in gently so as not to breakdown egg whites.

Butter a 2-quart souffle dish and sprinkle parmesan cheese on bottom and sides. Put a collar of wax paper around dish.

Pour mixture into dish and bake for 30 minutes. Turn off oven and leave it in for another 15 minutes. **Do not open oven door.** Serve at once with mushroom sauce on page 79.

Mushroom Sauce

For Cheese Souffle

Makes 1½ cups

2 tablespoons butter
1 small onion, chopped fine
1 tablespoon flour
1 cup chicken broth
8 mushrooms, sliced thinly
1 tablespoon lemon juice
¼ cup sherry, dry
   salt and pepper to taste

In a saucepan, melt 1 tablespoon butter; add onion. Cook over medium heat for about 3 minutes. Stir in flour. Gradually add broth, stirring with a wire whisk until smooth. Reduce heat to low and hold.

In a skillet, melt 1 tablespoon butter, add lemon juice and saute mushrooms. Add to sauce and let simmer for about 15 minutes. Season with salt and pepper to taste. Add sherry and cook for about 5 minutes more.

This classic New England dinner is always a favorite in my home, and it is so easy to prepare. Try it.

Corned Beef and Cabbage

1 4 to 5 lb. corned beef
6 medium potatoes
4 sliced carrots
1 large cabbage
4 peppercorns
1 bay leaf

Put corned beef into a large pot with bay leaf and peppercorns and cover with cold water. Bring to a boil; immediately reduce heat, and simmer for 3½ to 4 hours. Add peeled potatoes and carrots one hour before end of cooking time

In another pot cook wedges of cabbage in salted boiling water for 15 minutes or until tender.

Remove cabbage and drain. Remove meat and potatoes and drain. Arrange on a platter and serve with mustard.

What a divine entree for a super dinner. Serve it with any kind of potatoes and steamed vegetables. (I use mashed potatoes piped through a pastry bag.)

Crown Roast of Lamb

Order roast from your butcher, cut small slits in the lamb and insert slivers of garlic. Sprinkle lemon juice and pat roast with rosemary. Salt and pepper roast generously.

Preheat oven at 300°. Cover tips of roast with foil to prevent bones from burning while the roast cooks.

Place roast in a roasting pan and cook 25 minutes per pound.

Glaze (optional):

> 2 tablespoons brown sugar
> ½ cup mint jelly
> 2 tablespoons orange juice

Put all ingredients in a pan and cook for five minutes until it starts to caramelize. Glaze can be made ahead of time — if it thickens too much put over a flame for a few minutes. Serve separately in a gravy boat.

Duck a l'Orange

Serves 4 - 6

4 or 5 lb. duckling, prepared ready to cook
salt and pepper to taste
powdered sage
1 cup dry white wine
1 navel orange, bright color
4 tablespoons sugar
¼ cup wine vinegar
1 cup Veloute sauce
2 tablespoons Madeira
½ cup orange juice
1 tablespoon orange liqueur

Preheat oven to 425°. Season cavity of duck with salt, pepper and sage. Either truss the duckling or place on a vertical roaster in a shallow roasting pan. With a knife-point, pierce skin around thighs, back and lower breast. If not using the vertical roaster, place duckling on a rack in roasting pan. Roast at 425° for 15 minutes; reduce heat to 350°, and continue to roast for about one hour.

Peel orange part only from skin of orange and cut into thin strips. Reserve. Also reserve peeled orange for garnish.

When duck has roasted, remove from pan and place on a serving dish; turn off heat of oven, and place duck into oven with door ajar.

From roasting pan, remove all but about 1 tablespoon of grease from cooking juices. Add one cup dry white wine to juices; stir and reserve.

In a saucepan, combine the sugar and vinegar, and heat until mixture becomes somewhat syrupy. Add the wine-cooking juices mixture, and reduce volume to about one cup. Add the Veloute Sauce, Madeira, orange juice, orange liqueur and the orange strips. Reduce heat and simmer for a few minutes. Strain into a serving bowl through a fine sieve, and serve hot with the duckling. Garnish with orange sections.

VELOUTE SAUCE

2 tablespoons butter
2 tablespoons flour
1 cup chicken broth
 salt and pepper to taste

In a heavy saucepan, melt butter and add the flour. Whisk until smooth, and cook this 'roux' for a few minutes, but do not let it burn. Gradually add the chicken broth, whisking well after each addition; and let sauce cook until slightly thickened. Add salt and pepper to taste.

Chicken Marsala

Serves 6

12 pieces of chicken (cuts of your choice)
 3 tablespoons olive oil
 2 garlic cloves, finely chopped
 2 cups stewed tomatoes
 dash of paprika
 ¼ teaspoon basil
 ¼ teaspoon oregano
 ¼ teaspoon rosemary
 ½ cup marsala dry wine
 salt and pepper to taste

In a large skillet, or saute pan, heat the garlic with the oil and a dash of salt. Saute the chicken till golden brown. Discard the oil. Add tomatoes, herbs and marsala. Cover and simmer for about an hour. Serve with white rice.

We first had the pleasure of trying this most delicious dish at the home of Dr. and Mrs. Thomas Doan. The occasion was a brunch in honor of President Miguel Aleman of Mexico. Duke had one bite of this south-of-the-border dish and flipped. Rue (a beautiful blonde; my son Ethan's first "crush," and a great cook) graciously gave me the recipe. Rue is now Mrs. Robert Byars.

From that day, this became Duke's favorite dish, and he would carry the recipe with him wherever he went. Sometimes he would call me from Africa or Europe and ask me questions like, "how much cheese?" or "what temperature?" I always got a kick out of this.

This became one of his "two most favorite recipes." The other one being "Hominy Grits Souffle" which recipe is in this book, also.

Duke's Souffle

1 lb. grated cheddar cheese
1 lb. grated jack cheese
2 cans diced chiles (it really depends on
   your taste; if you like it hotter, add more chiles)
   (Duke liked this casserole extremely hot,
   so we used two large cans of chiles!)
4 eggs
1 medium size can stewed tomatoes, drained

Preheat oven to 325°.

Butter a deep casserole. Make layers of cheeses and chiles. Separate eggs. Beat egg whites until stiff. Beat egg yolks and fold into egg whites. Gently pour the egg mixture over, covering the cheeses and chiles and oozed through with a fork. Bake for half an hour. Add drained tomatoes; pushing them down with a fork. Bake for another half hour.

Outrageously delicious!

Filet Mignon aux Champignons

1 tablespoon butter
1 tablespoon cooking oil
4 filet mignon
3 tablespoons chopped red onions
2 tablespoons flour
1 small can sliced mushroom caps (drained)
2 tablespoons dry sherry
1 cup beef bouillon (cube is alright)
½ teaspoons "Kitchen Bouquet" (browning agent)
2 teaspoons Herbes de Provence (page 42)
   garlic powder, salt and black pepper
      to taste

About 30 minutes before cooking, prepare your filets as follows: Lay them on a wooden board. Rub a few drops of oil on each of them, salt, pepper, garlic powder and a sprinkle of Herbes de Provence, press and rub into meat. Repeat on other side.

In a skillet, melt butter and add oil, when hot, brown filets on both sides. Remove to a warm platter. To the same skillet add the onions and saute them. Add the flour, stir and cook for about one minute. Add the mushrooms, the sherry and enough bouillon to reach a creamy consistency and stir in the "Kitchen Bouquet." Return filets to the skillet and reheat thoroughly. Arrange filets on serving platter, cover them with the sauce, and serve with rice and steamed fresh vegetables.

"Ambrosia" (nectar of the gods) is owned by Geril and Gosta Muller and is probably one of the most fabulous restaurants I have had the pleasure to dine in. From the moment you walk in, you are in a world of red velvet and crystal chandeliers with divine violins.

The cuisine is incredible and the service impecable. I was estatic when I received these three unique recipes from "Ambrosia," and I would like to share them with you.

Piquant Gravlax with Mustard Sauce

1 tablespoon fresh dill, finely chopped
3 tablespoons salt
4 teaspoons sugar
¼ teaspoon freshly ground black pepper
¼ teaspoon ground allspice
¼ cup red or white wine vinegar
2 lbs. fresh whole salmon filet with skin on
  center piece - the best cut

Sprinkle a little dill in the bottom of a flat dish (such as a glass casserole) that the salmon fits into compactly. Set salmon skin down in dish; sprinkle with remaining dill. Blend salt, sugar, pepper and allspice, distributing evenly over salmon and patting onto flesh. Pour vinegar over fish.

Cover dish with clear plastic film and set a weight on the dish - such as a plate holding a pound of butter or a large bottle of juice. Refrigerate at least two days; spoon juices over fish occasionally during this time. After a day, remove the weights. The salmon keeps as long as a week in the brine, but gradually grows too salty to be enjoyable.

Slice fish across the grain on a diagonal to the skin; cut away from the skin. Makes 4 to 6 main dish servings or 8 to 12 first course servings.

Serve thin slices of Gravlax alone or on bread as an appetizer. Decorate with fresh dill sprigs and lemon; or slice a little thicker as main dish and served with new hot boiled potatoes and creamed spinach and mustard sauce.

MUSTARD SAUCE

Stir together 2 tablespoons Dijon mustard, 1 tablespoon sugar, 1½ tablespoon wine vinegar, ½ teaspoon salt and 1 teaspoon finely chopped fresh dill, gradually and smoothly beat in 1/3 cup salad oil. Makes about 2/3 cup.

Happy dining from Ambrosia.

This recipe was given to me by a friend who does not like to cook.

Chicken Cacciatori

12 pieces of chicken, all parts
1 jar of Italian cooking tomato sauce

Place chicken in a baking dish and pour sauce over it. Preheat oven to 400° and bake for 1 hour.

That's it!

Filet of Veal Zurichoise

Serves 12

1¾ lb. veal filet
1 onion, minced
¾ stick butter, unsalted
1 lb. mushrooms, sliced
1 cup dry white wine
3 tablespoons lemon juice
½ teaspoon Worcestershire sauce
1 cup heavy cream
1½ tablespoons flour
1½ tablespoons butter, softened
   salt and pepper
3 tablespoons vegetable oil

In a stainless steel or enameled skillet cook 1 onion, minced, in ¾ stick (6 tablespoons) unsalted butter over moderate heat, stirring until it is softened, add 1 lb. mushrooms, sliced and saute the mixture over moderately high heat, stirring for 1 to 2 minutes, or until the mushrooms are golden. Add 1 cup dry white wine, 3 tablespoons lemon juice, and ½ teaspoon Worcestershire sauce, bring the liquid to a boil, and boil the mixture for 2 minutes. Transfer the mushrooms with a slotted spoon to a bowl and whisk into the skillet bits of beurre manie, made by kneading together 1½ teaspoons each of flour and softened unsalted butter, until the mixture is thickened. Stir in 1 cup heavy cream and simmer the mixture, stirring, for 4-minutes, or until it is thickened slightly. Add the mushrooms, beat the mixture, stirring until the mushrooms are heated through and season the sauce with salt and pepper. Keep the sauce warm.

Cut a 1¾ pound veal filet crosswise into 24 slices and pat the slices dry. Sprinkle the veal slices with salt and pepper and dredge them in flour, shaking off excess. In a large heavy skillet, saute the veal in batches, in 3 tablespoons vegetable oil, over moderately high heat for 1 to 2 minutes on each side, or until it is golden and springy to the touch. Transfer the veal as it is cooked with a slotted spatula to heated platter, arranging the slices decoratively, and spoon the sauce over it. Garnish the dish with minced fresh parsley leaves and serve it with noodles.

So easy and great to look at!

Glamorous Meat Loaf

1½ lb. ground beef
½ cup chopped onion
2 eggs
1 cup tomato sauce
1 cup bread crumbs
1 ripe banana
mashed potatoes (4 servings)

Mix all ingredients (except mashed potatoes) well and bake for 1 hour at 325°.

After your meatloaf is done, transfer onto a platter and let all the juices run out. Discard juices. In a pastry bag with a No. 6 star tip, swirl mashed potatoes evenly over the entire meatloaf. Put under broiler until top stars turn golden brown.

One of the very first people I met when I first arrived in Los Angeles was Duke's secretary Mary St. John, Mary worked for Duke for 28 years. A striking brunette, full of life. Mary has the wonderful quality of making people happy and at ease. Duke always told me she was the greatest and would not know what to do without her.

Well, I fell in love with her instantly, she took me under her wing, and every moment I have spent with her has been a pleasure.

The first time she invited me for lunch she asked me to pick a restaurant of my choice. I told her I would like to go to "Der Wienerschnitzel," I had to wait till she finished laughing to explain to her that we did not have Hot Dogs in Lima and that Duke was always taking me to fancy restaurants and that I was dying for those wonderful American sandwiches called Hot Dogs.

She was my matron of honor at our wedding and she is also my daughter Aissa's godmother. Till today I love her dearly and treasure her friendship.

I was a terrible cook then, literally, I could not boil water. I remember when we were all in Honolulu while Duke was filming a movie called "In Harms Way" with Patricia Neal. I had nothing to do this afternoon, so I decided to do some cooking. When Mary and Duke walked in from location there was a chicken hanging in the kitchen. I explained to the startled faces that the recipe called for chicken drippings, I still have not lived this one down.

Here are some delightful recipes she served at her home on different occasions.

Look for pages 91 and 138.

Lobster Casserole

     1 lb. lobster meat
  1¾ cups bread crumbs, toasted
  1¼ cups milk
     2 eggs
     ¼ teaspoon dry mustard
        salt to taste
        dash cayenne pepper

Dice lobster meat. Mix with all ingredients (other than topping). Spoon into one casserole or individual baking shells.

Add topping. Bake in a 375° preheated oven for 30 minutes or until topping is golden brown.

Topping:

  1¾ cups toasted bread crumbs
  ½ cup melted butter

Note:

For a creamier consistency, light cream may be used instead of milk.

Lobster Thermidor "Villa Fontana"

Serves 2

2 pounds lobster, cooked
2 ounces melted butter
4 mushrooms, sliced
1 tablespoon minced shallot
¼ cup Sauterne
½ cup heavy cream
1½ tablespoons grated Parmesan cheese
½ cup fish stock (clam juice may be used)
1 heaping tablespoon flour
1 cup mashed potatoes
1 egg yolk
salt and white pepper to taste

Cut lobster in half from head to tail, being very careful to not damage the shell, Take all the meat out carefully, and cut into ½ inch cubes. Clean shell under running water.

Place a bit of the melted butter in a hot skillet. Add the mushrooms, shallot, and 1 minute later, the lobster meat. Stir constantly. Then, add the sauterne and ¼ cup of the cream. Reduce the liquid by half. Add ½ tablespoon of Parmesan cheese. Add fish stock and bring to a boil. Mix flour with remaining melted butter. Stir this "roux" slowly into hot lobster mixture until it becomes a creamy and thick sauce. Season with salt and white pepper.

Squeeze mashed potatoes from a pastry bag fitted with a large star tip along the lobster shell from head to tail. Place lobster mixture inside the shell. Beat remaining cream and mix with egg yolk, and pour it over the lobster meat. Sprinkle with remaining Parmesan cheese and place lobster under broiler, or salamander, to brown. Serve hot.

Miniature Hungarian Cabbage Rolls

Makes 50 Rolls

1 large head of cabbage
1 egg
½ lb. ground beef
¼ lb. pork sausage
¼ cup onion, finely chopped
¼ cup raw rice
¼ cup milk
¾ teaspoon seasoned salt
¼ teaspoon seasoned pepper
1 package Lawry's Goulash Seasoning Mix
1 1 lb. can tomatoes
1 8-ounce can tomato sauce

Separate cabbage leaves and immerse in boiling water for about 1 minute (until softened). Beat egg. Add ground beef, pork sausage, onion, rice, milk, salt, pepper, and 1 tablespoon goulash seasoning mix.Mix thoroughly. Blend remaining goulash seasoning mix, tomatoes, and tomato sauce in a sauce pan. Bring to a boil. Reduce heat and simmer 15 to 20 minutes. Cut softened cabbage leaves in pieces about 4 x 4 inches, removing the center rib. Place about ½ tablespoon meat mixture on cabbage leaf. Roll up securely. Place in a large, buttered, shallow baking dish. Pour tomato mixture on top of the cabbage rolls. Cover and bake at 350° for 25 to 30 minutes.

Having to work in between chefs became quite a bit of fun, especially working with my tennis buddy Eddie Nedo. Eddie has her own catering company and is a super cook, and I have learned so much from her. Her manicotti is heavenly and light, you can also use pasta shells — but I prefer the crepes.

Manicotti with Crepes

Tomato Sauce:

> 1/4 cup olive oil
> 1 cup chopped white onion
> 2 cloves garlic
> 1 2 lb. 3 oz. can Italian tomatoes
> 6 ounces canned tomato paste
> 1-1/2 cups water
> 2 tablespoons chopped fresh parsley
> 2 teaspoons sugar
> 1 teaspoon oregano
> 1/2 teaspoon dried basil
> 1 tablespoon salt
> pepper to taste
> 24 Crepes (see page 130)

Filling for crepes:

> 2 lbs. ricotta cheese
> 8 ounces mozzarella cheese, grated
> 1/3 cup parmesan cheese, grated
> 2 eggs
> 1 tablespoon chopped fresh parsley
> 1 tablespoon salt
> pepper to taste

Saute the onions in oil. Add garlic when onions are golden brown. Add tomatoes and tomato paste. Continue cooking. Add parsley, sugar, oregano, basil, salt and pepper. Add water and cook until slightly thick.

Mix together all of the ingredients. **To assemble:** spoon layers of tomato sauce on the bottom of one 13" x 9" x 2" baking dish. In center of each crepe, place about ¼ cup filling and roll up. Place crepes, seam down, in single layer in baking dish. Cover with rest of sauce and sprinkle with 2 tablespoons parmesan. Bake uncovered in a 350° oven for 30 minutes.

Through my years at the restaurant, I made many a delightful friend. One of them is Roy Pingo. Roy is a number one connoisseur of food. As a matter of fact, he teaches cooking and he has written two books of his own, "Gourmet Plus International" and "The Eggs Act."

I got to know Roy well one evening. My brother-in-law asked me to help him arrange a surprise party to celebrate my sister's and his 20th wedding anniversary. I love parties so I was delighted. I ordered the music, called the caterers, ordered the flowers, etc., etc.

The guests started to arrive and everything was going great. An hour went by and no caterers. I really started to worry. So I went to the phone and called the caterers. To my horror, she said to me in ever-so-perfect English, "but Mrs. Wayne, you said next Saturday!" There was no point in arguing! I slowly hung up the phone and immediately made my way through the crowd to Roy, who without batting an eyelash, said, "I need 20 dozen eggs!"

The party was a success. Roy's variety of omelets was a hit. What I would have done without him, I don't know. Here are three delightful recipes from Master Pingo. (pages 96-66-54)

Paella

4 ounces butter	Serves 6 - 8
2 tablespoons olive oil	
1 medium size onion, chopped	
2 lbs. boned chicken breasts, skinned and cut into 1" strips	
2 cups long grain rice	
1 teaspoon saffron, crushed	

4 cups chicken broth
salt and pepper to taste
3 Chorizo sausages, cooked, sliced
(or any preferred sausage)
4 ounces sweet, red peppers, chopped

Two or three of the following kinds of fish or seafood:

18 large, shelled, deveined shrimp, raw
(sauteed in butter until pink)
18 small clams, scrubbed, left in shells
18 mussels, scrubbed, left in shells
4 lobster tails, cleaned, cut into chunks
(split shell but leave meat in shell)
18 scallops (sauteed in butter)
2 pounds fish fillets (sauteed in butter)
4 tablespoons chopped, fresh parsley

In paella pan, melt butter and add oil. Add onion and saute until softened. Add chicken and cook until light brown, turning once or twice. Remove chicken and set aside. Add rice to pan and cook for about 10 minutes. Do not brown; add more butter if necessary. Stir in saffron. Add chicken broth and bring to boil; reduce heat to simmer. Add salt and pepper to taste, and simmer, uncovered, for 20 minutes, or until rice is tender.

Add any of the sauteed fish or seafood to pan and very gently mix. Return chicken to pan; add cooked sausage and peppers to pan, and gently mix. Add more broth if mixture is dry. Serve hot, garnished with parsley. Two cups of small cooked green peas may also be added.

For the clams, mussels or lobster tails:

Add these on top of the finished paella dish; then bake it at 400 ° just long enough until the clams or mussels open, and the lobster tails turn a red color, which should only take a few minutes. Be certain to discard any clams or mussels which do not open.

In 1965 when Duke was working in Durango, Mexico filming a western called "Sons of Katie Elder" with Dean Martin and directed by Henry Hathaway, we sure got to eat a lot of delicious Italian food, thanks to Dean's mother, who would send from Los Angeles all kinds of goodies. One night Dean invited us to have dinner at his table, his mother had just sent him a big pot of Pasta Fasul, it was almost freezing and the dish was hot and delicious. I told Dean how delicious I thought it was. A couple of days later I received a letter from Dean's mother with the recipe. I was thrilled. It has a few calories, but who is counting.

Pasta Fasul

In boiling, salted water cook 2 cups of small elbow macaroni (pasta) until tender. Drain, and mix with 2 cups of Progresso white kidney beans with liquid. To this mixture add 1 cup of water.

In a frying pan, saute 1 onion and (if desired) ½ bud of garlic, thinly sliced, in ½ cup of olive oil until onion is soft and light brown.

Add the olive oil and onion sauce to the bean and pasta mixture, salt and pepper to taste, then simmer until it is the consistency of thick soup. If it becomes too thick, it can be thinned out with additional water.

Serve with hot French bread and a salad.

This is a terrific summer entree! You can also use it as an appetizer by slicing it into smaller pieces. This is one of Peru's favorite dishes.

Peruvian Causa

 2 13 ounce cans tuna or albacore
    chunk light, water pack
 1 red onion, large, coarsely chopped
 3 tablespoons red wine vinegar
1/4 cup lemon juice
    salt and pepper to taste
 4 large russet potatoes
1/3 cup vegetable oil
 1 head Boston lettuce
 2 hard-boiled eggs, sliced
 1 avocado, sliced
24 black olives, pitted
 2 tablespoons lemon juice for potatoes
    mayonnaise

Drain tuna and mix with onion and enough mayonnaise to hold together. Season with ¼ cup lemon juice, red wine vinegar, salt and pepper. Refrigerate. This is your salad mixture.

Cook potatoes, whole in their skins, until soft. Peel and mash while still hot. Add salt to taste. Let cool. Add vegetable oil and lemon juice. Work dough with your hands. Make a 1-inch thick layer of potatoes and place on a round platter. This should be about half of the potato mixture. Cover with the salad and top with a second layer of potatoes. By now it should look like a cake, ready to be frosted. Cover entire Causa with a thin layer of mayonnaise. Garnish all around with lettuce. Top with egg and avocado slices and olives. I usually put a tomato rose on the top for color.

Another delicacy from "Ambrosia."

Filet de Poisson Blanc poche

Avec Brie a la Nouvelle

Poached Filet of fresh White Fish with Brie

Filet of fresh white fish poached in fish stock - Chablis and Pernod, topped with thin slices of Brie - served in Creme-Fraiche Sauce.

INGREDIENTS: Per person.

- 5 - 6 ounces Fresh White Fish
  (sole or other fresh fish)
- ½ teaspoon Shallot Onions, chopped
- 3 ounces Fish stock
- 3 ounces Chablis (or other dry white wine)
- ½ ounce Pernod
- 4 ounces Creme-Fraiche
- 2 thin slices of fresh Brie cheese

Lightly butter skillet. Place fresh fish skin down. Spread top of fish with shallot onions, add fish stock, and place on open burner. When hot add Chablis and cover with lid. Reduce to light boiling for 3 minutes. Remove lid and top fish with Brie and poach for two more minutes under lid. Sprinkle fish with Pernod and remove fish to warm platter.

Reduce cooking liquid 1/3 and add Creme-Fraiche. Bring to a boil for about 1 minute, add a little Pernod to taste, and strain the sauce into a warm sauce boat.

To serve:

Put sauce on the plate to cover bottom. Place fish on top. Decorate with tomato rose bud and fresh dill. Garnish as you like with al dente cooked fresh vegetables in season.

Creme Fraiche

> 1 quart Whipping Cream
> 1/3 cup Buttermilk

Mix well and leave overnight in warm room temperature.

BON APPETIT!

Party Chicken

Serves 8

> 8 chicken breast halves
> 8 slices bacon
> 4 ounces chipped beef (package)
> 1 can undiluted mushroom soup
> ½ pint sour cream

Wrap each chicken breast neatly with a slice of bacon, going around the chicken breast, lengthwise. Secure with a toothpick, if necessary.

Butter a baking dish and scatter chipped beef over bottom. Arrange chicken on top of beef.

Mix soup and sour cream, and pour overall.

325° for 2 hours, uncovered.

Great with new potatoes and steamed vegetables.

Poached Salmon with Dill Weed Cream Sauce

Serves 4

1 cup water
1 small stalk celery
1 medium carrot
1 medium onion
1 bay leaf
2 cloves
1 sprig parsley
6 peppercorns
1 pinch each: thyme, basil, sage and dill weed
salt and pepper
4 salmon steaks

For the Cream Sauce:

⅛ lb. soft butter
1½ tablespoons flour
½ cup dry white wine
½ cup light cream
1 teaspoon dill weed
salt and pepper

In a large skillet, combine all ingredients except salmon steaks; bring to a boil, simmer for 12 minutes. Add salmon, cover and simmer for 10 minutes (as a general rule, fish should be cooked 10 minutes per inch thick). Remove from pan and keep warm on a hot platter. Make beurre manie, which is the combination of the soft butter and the flour mixed together in a paste-like consistency, then add it to the liquid, stir well, cook gently for 3 minutes, then add wine, light cream, dill weed and salt and pepper. Simmer for 5 minutes and adjust consistency if needed by adding more wine or cream if too thick. A few moments before serving, place salmon steaks back into the cream sauce and heat thoroughly, but do not boil.

Serve with a wedge of lemon on side of dish.

Duke came home from his location for "True Grit" with this recipe, given to him by director Henry Hathaway. Apparently, Henry had fixed it one night and delighted everyone with it. My friendship with the Hathaways goes way back. Skip, (Mrs. Hathaway), is my son Ethan's godmother, and we've been to many locations together and had a ball! Duke won the Oscar award for best actor for his performance in "True Grit," directed, I am very happy to say, by Mr. Henry Hathaway.

Pork Chops and Sauerkraut

Serves 4

1 tablespoon oil or butter
4 pork chops ¾ inch thick, trimmed
1 jar sauerkraut, 8-ounces, drained
1 teaspoon caraway seed
1 pint sour cream, room temperature
   paprika

Preheat oven to 350°. Heat oil or butter in large skillet over medium-high heat. Add chops and brown well, turning once, about 3 to 4 minutes each side. Transfer to baking dish. Divide sauerkraut evenly over chops and sprinkle with caraway. Top each with ½ cup sour cream. Sprinkly generously with paprika. Bake until topping is golden, about 25 to 30 minutes. Serve immediately.

This Quesadilla was very popular at the restaurant.

I love Mexican food and could eat it every day if it had no calories.

You will enjoy this recipe.

Quesadillas

Serves 4

4 chicken breasts "white meat", boiled, with skin and bone removed, diced into medium sized pieces
6 cups Jack cheese, grated
1 cup tomato, diced into small pieces
1 4 ounce can green chiles
(half chile per quesadilla)
¼ cup white onion diced very fine
4 medium flour tortillas
1 small can Ortega Salsa

In ungreased grill or pan on high heat . . . spread cheese over the tortilla, add onions and chiles until cheese is melting then add chicken and tomatoes.

Fold Quesadilla in half turning frequently until browned lightly and the cheese melted thoroughly with other ingredients.

Serve topped with Guacamole (see page 25) and 2 tablespoons salsa.

TONY POPE'S POTATO BOAT

LOBSTER BISQUE

TOMATO ROSE

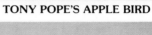

TONY POPE'S APPLE BIRD

TERRY'S HORS D'OEUVRE DOLL

POTATO BASKET

107

POPOVERS

108

Selecting your roast is very important. Prime beef will be expensive, but the end result will make it well worth it.

Roast Prime Beef with Gravy

1 roast beef
½ stick butter
1 carrot, cut in half
1 celery, cut in thirds
1 onion, cut in half
6 sprigs parsley
garlic powder
seasoned salt
1 teaspoon Herbes de Provence (page 42)
salt, fresh ground pepper
1 cup red wine
1 cup water

Preheat oven to 400 °.
Rub roast on all sides with garlic powder, seasoned salt, ground pepper and a small amount of salt. Place in a greased roasting pan using ½ stick butter, sprinkle the Herbes de Provence on top, surround the vegetables and put in oven. After cooking for 15 minutes, reduce temperature to 325°, and add half the amount of water in the pan. Multiply the weight of the roast by 20 minutes, and this will give you the cooking time. About half way through cooking period, douse one-half the red wine over roast and keep adding through rest of cooking time, and the same with water on bottom of pan. When cooked, take out of oven and allow to rest for 20 minutes before carving.

GRAVY:

> 1½ tablespoons flour
> 1½ cups water
>   salt, pepper
> ¼ teaspoon Kitchen Bouquet

Place roasting pan on top of stove plate, remove vegetables, heat beef fat and juices on medium-high temperature, then add combination of flour and water, previously mixed in a measuring cup, stir constantly until it thickens. Add ¼ teaspoon Kitchen Bouquet and stir. Serve on top of roast slices if desired.

Three "C" Casserole

(Corn, Crackers and Cheese)

> 2 cups creamed corn, canned
> 1 cup crushed soda crackers
> ½ cup chopped celery
> ¼ cup chopped onion
> 1 cup grated cheddar cheese
> 1 teaspoon salt
> ¼ teaspoon paprika
> 2 eggs, beaten
> 1½ cups milk
> 2 tablespoons melted butter

Mix all ingredients. Pour into an 8-cup casserole and bake at 350° for one hour.

Simple as ABC . . . and so delicious.

Texas was one of the places we always enjoyed visiting. Duke felt at home there. The people and the parties were always great! Whether it was a back yard barbeque or a black tie sit down dinner, they were always beautiful and fun.

Texans seem to have more than just southern hospitality; they have a charisma all their own. Any place you go, you will find the people extremely friendly and outgoing.

Duke made two great motion pictures in Texas: "The Alamo", and "The Hellfighters", so we spent quite a bit of time there and made lots of friends. My sister, Josephine Stinson, lives in Dallas with her husband and children, so I always have the opportunity to return. Of all the wonderful recipes I have collected, I will share with you two typically southern ones; Hominy Grits Souffle, and this delicious home-made Chili.

Texas Chili

5 lbs. lean beef, cubed or coarsely ground
1 quart water
3 tablespoons sugar
2½ tablespoons salt
6 ounces olive oil
5 tablespoons flour
6-8 tablespoons pure ground chili
5 cloves garlic
1 teaspoon pepper
2 teaspoons oregano
1 teaspoon curry

In a large pot, combine water, meat, sugar, and salt; bring to a boil, skim, then reduce heat immediately to a simmer. Do not let boil again. In a skillet, heat oil, add flour, stir and cook for 2 minutes without browning. Add garlic and spices to oil mixture, cook briefly, then add entire mixture to meat. Simmer meat for about 1½ hours until meat is very tender.

An incredible entree. A work of art! Definitely a must for a very special occasion!

Ring of Sole with Spinach and Salmon Mousse

Serves 6 to 8

Sauce Mornay:
>   3 tablespoons butter
>   2 shallots, minced
>   5 tablespoons flour
>   1 cup milk at room temperature
>   4 egg yolks
>   dash of nutmeg
>   salt and pepper to taste

Spinach Mousse:
>   1 10-ounce package frozen chopped spinach
>   thawed and drained
>   1 tablespoon green onion tops, minced
>   ½ teaspoon nutmeg
>   2 egg whites
>   pinch of cream of tartar
>   pinch of salt and pepper

Salmon Mousse:
>   1 pound fresh salmon,
>   boned, skinned and finely ground
>   1 tablespoon fresh dill, minced or
>   1½ teaspoons dried dill weed
>   1 teaspoon paprika
>   2 egg whites
>   pinch each of salt and cream of tartar
> 8 or 9 sole fillets

To make sauce Mornay:
Melt the butter in saucepan. Add shallots. Saute until golden brown. Add flour. Remove from heat. Add milk and stir. Cook over low heat, stirring often until thickened. Remove from heat. In another bowl, beat the egg yolks. Add a little of the sauce to the egg yolks. Then add the yolks to the rest of the sauce. Mix well. Return to heat for one minute. Add the salt, pepper, and nutmeg. Set aside.

To make Spinach Mousse:
Mix together the drained spinach, half of the Mornay Sauce, onions and nutmeg. Beat the egg whites until foamy, add the salt and cream of tartar. Continue beating until stiff; fold into the spinach mixture. Add salt and pepper to taste. Set aside.

To make Salmon Mousse:
Mix together the salmon, the remaining Mornay Sauce, dill, lemon juice and paprika. Beat the egg whites until foamy; add the salt and cream of tartar. Continue beating until stiff, and fold into the salmon mixture. Set aside.

Assembly:
Preheat oven to 350°. Rinse sole fillets in salted water. Slightly flatten the fillets with a rolling pin that has been moistened. (A moistened mallet will do.) Butter an 8 or 9 cup ring mold. Set the fillets in the mold, skinned or darker side up. Slightly overlap them. Let small end of each hang over the center of the mold. Let wide end extend over outside edge. Spread the Spinach Mousse carefully on the fillets. Then spread the Salmon Mousse on the Spinach Mousse. Fold the edges of the fillets back over. Cover with buttered wax paper. Place the ring mold in roasting pan half-filled with water, and bake 40 to 45 minutes. Remove from oven and turn out onto a platter. Blot any excess liquid. Slice and serve hot.

One of my favorite recipes. It is delicate in taste; it's beautiful to look at. I usually serve it for lunch as the main course or in smaller portions as an appetizer for a formal dinner.

Salmon Mousse with Cucumber Sauce

```
     2  15-½ ounce cans of red salmon, drained
or  1½  pounds poached fresh salmon
     2  envelopes unflavored gelatin
     ½  cup cold water
     1  cup boiling water
     ½  cup mayonnaise (I use low-cal)
     4  tablespoons finely chopped white onion
     3  tablespoons lemon juice
     1  teaspoon tabasco
        dash of cayenne
     1  teaspoon salt
     ½  pint whipping cream
        a few drops of red food coloring, if desired
```

Discard skin and bones from salmon. In a large bowl place the cold water. Add the gelatin and let stand for a few minutes until it softens. Add boiling water and with a wooden spoon swirl it until gelatin disolves. Add the salmon, mayonnaise, onion, lemon juice, tabasco, cayenne and salt. Mix thoroughly. Puree mixture until silky and smooth.

Whip the cream until soft peaks form and fold gently into the salmon mixture. Pour into a 6-cup fish-shaped mold, cover with plastic wrap and refrigerate until set; about 3 hours. If you need the mousse in a hurry you can freeze it for about

20 minutes and then refrigerate for about an hour. (It can be kept frozen for two weeks.)

Garnish with Bibb lettuce, green olives, pimientos and cucumber slices. Serve cold with cucumber sauce.

Cucumber Sauce

1 very large or 2 medium cucumbers
1 cup sour cream
1 teaspoon white pepper and salt to taste
1 tablespoon sweet pickle relish
1 tablespoon plus 1 teaspoon white vinegar
1 teaspoon sugar, if desired

Trim ends and peel cucumbers. Slice lengthwise into quarters and discard seeds. Shred cucumbers using hand grater or shredder blade of food processor. Place shredded cucumbers in a strainer and let stand 30 minutes. Squeeze out any remaining juice. Place cucumbers in a small bowl. Stir in remaining ingredients until blended. May be refrigerated up to 2 days.

Sole Mousse with Lobster Newburg

1½ lbs. sole fillets
4 tablespoons butter
½ cup flour
¾ teaspoon salt
3 cups light cream
1/3 cup dry sherry
1 3-ounce can whole mushrooms, drained
1 tablespoon catsup
2 egg yolks
2 cups cooked lobster meat
1½ teaspoons salt
⅛ teaspoon white pepper
2 egg whites

Rinse sole and dry with paper towels. Cut each fillet into about 6 pieces. Put through a meat grinder using the finest blade 4 times. Or, puree with a food processor using the steel knife blade. Place in the large bowl of an electric mixer. Refrigerate, covered, for 30 minutes. Generously grease a 2-quart metal Charlotte mold, 7" in diameter. Refrigerate.

Meanwhile, make lobster filling. Melt butter in a medium saucepan. Remove from heat. Stir in ¼ cup flour and ¾ teaspoon salt until well blended. Gradually stir in 1 cup of cream. Bring to a boil, stirring constantly. Reduce heat and simmer for 1 minute; stir in mushrooms and catsup. Cook over medium heat until hot. Beat egg yolks with ¼ cup cream, and stir into sauce; add lobster, and cook for 1 minute, stirring. Remove from heat.

Add ¼ cup flour, 1½ teaspoons salt and pepper to sole. Blend well. With electric beater at medium speed, beat in egg whites. Gradually beat in the 2 cups of cream, about 2 tablespoons at a time, which will take about 15 minutes. Mixture should be smooth and stiff.

Preheat oven to 325°.

Set aside 1 cup of the sole mixture. Use remaining mixture to line bottom and sides of prepared mold to within 1" of top. Reserve 1 cup lobster filling and refrigerate. Use remaining filling to fill the lined mold. Cover with reserved sole mixture, spreading to edge of mold. Cover mold loosely with buttered wax paper. Place into a roasting pan; pour hot water to a 2" level around mold. Bake 45 to 50 minutes or until firm at edge when gently pressed with fingertips.

About 10 minutes before mousse is done, heat the 1 cup of reserved lobster filling over hot water.

Loosen mousse around sides with a small spatula or knife. Invert onto a heated serving platter; lift off mold. Spoon heated filling over top. Garnish with watercress and slices of lemon, if desired. Cut into wedges and serve.

Marvelous!

When I first opened the restaurant, my mom gave me the recipe for her fabulous Spinach Pie. I find it simply delicious, and I guess so did a lot of other people because we had so many customers coming back for it. It became a regular on our menu and we must have made a million of them.

I had a waiter who worked for me for almost three years, quite a wonderful guy. I could almost sense it when he was hungry. Everytime we asked him, "Louie, what would you like to eat?" he would say, "Spinach Pie, please." I would say to him, "but you are going to turn green from eating so much Spinach Pie; please try something else." He would reply, "no, I like Spinach Pie." Well, so do I . . . but not every day.

This is a real great pie for a bridge luncheon. Serve it with fresh fruits and you will definitely have a winner!

Spinach Pie

     1½ pounds packaged frozen chopped spinach
      4 eggs
     1½ pounds white sauce
         garlic salt to taste
         salt and pepper to taste
         dash nutmeg
      3 hard-boiled eggs, cut into sixths
         with an egg-wedger
      1 egg yolk mixed with 1 tablespoon water,
         for egg-wash
      2 recipes for Pastry Dough (page 167)

Thaw spinach and press out all of the moisture (very important), using a strainer, and place into a mixing bowl. Add the eggs, white sauce; garlic salt, salt, pepper and nutmeg.

118

Fit one recipe of Pastry Dough into a 9" pie dish. Trim any excess dough. Pour in the spinach mixture; arrange and press the wedges of eggs into the spinach mixture. Cover with the other recipe of Pastry Dough and press around edges to seal. Brush top with egg-wash. Make two "V" cuts into top of pie.

Bake at 375° for one hour. Let the pie cool for 10 minutes before serving.

Norwegian Fish Mousse

    3 lbs. fillet of haddock,
      or any firm white fish
    ¼ cup corn starch
    2 teaspoons salt
    ⅛ teaspoon nutmeg
    2 cups milk
    2 cups heavy cream

Rinse fish and cut into pieces. Puree in a food processor or blender. Transfer to a mixing bowl, add corn starch and nutmeg, and gradually beat in milk and cream, blending well. Spoon mixture into a buttered 1½-quart baking dish, or a lightly oiled ring mold. Cover with lightly buttered foil and set into a pan of hot water. Bake at 350° for 50 minutes or until firm.

Turn out molded mousse onto a warm platter. Garnish with shrimp sauce, curry sauce, or Bechamel sauce.

Best spaghetti sauce ever!

Spaghetti Sauce a la Milanese

2½ lbs. ground beef
5 tablespoons olive oil
2 large white onions, chopped
4 tablespoons flour
1 8-ounce can drained mushroom pieces
2 tablespoons finely chopped celery
1 6-ounce can tomato paste
1 16-ounce can peeled tomatoes
2 medium size tomatoes, diced
2 cups chicken broth
1½ cups Burgundy or Bordeaux
5 cloves garlic, mashed
¼ teaspoon basil*
¼ teaspoon sage*
¼ teaspoon thyme*
¼ teaspoon oregano*
¼ teaspoon curry powder
1 bay leaf
   salt and pepper to taste

In a skillet, saute meat until brown. Remove from heat and drain meat. Set aside.

In a large pot heat olive oil; add onions and cook until translucent and golden. Add meat to pot and add tomato paste, flour, salt and pepper and mix well. Reduce heat. Mash peeled tomatoes and add to meat mixture along with any tomato juice that remains in can. Add chicken broth, mushrooms, red wine, garlic, fresh tomatoes, celery, herbs, and bay leaf. Cover and simmer for at least 1½ hours, stirring occasionally.

Note:

I always freeze this sauce. It keeps very nicely.

*2 tablespoons of Italian herb mix can be used instead of individual herbs.

Just great anytime!

Spinach/Cottage Cheese Casserole

    3 eggs
    1 pint cottage cheese
    ¼ cup buttermilk (or milk with a little lemon)
    5 ounces sharp cheddar cheese (1½ cups)
    10 ounces packaged frozen spinach

Beat eggs lightly and add rest of the ingredients. Bake at 350°
for 45 minutes.

Swiss Onion Tart

    1 10″ pastry shell
    2 tablespoons butter
    1½ lbs. white onions, chopped
    1 tablespoon flour
    2 egg yolks, beaten
    1 cup heavy cream
      salt and pepper to taste
      dash of nutmeg

Preheat oven to 375°. On medium heat, melt butter in a skillet; add onions and let them cook ever so slowly until translucent and soft. Sprinkle flour over them; mix well and let
cook a while. Remove from heat and add the egg yolks. Then
gradually stir in cream; add salt and pepper and nutmeg. Pour
mixture into pastry shell. Bake 40 to 50 minutes or until filling
is firm.

Motion picture director Vincente Minnelli, who has delighted the world with his unbelievable talent, to my suprise is also a great gourmet cook. I accidentally found this out while having lunch with his wife, Lee. I told Lee I just had to have one of his recipes for my new cook book. Vincente graciously consented.

One of my favorite motion pictures in the whole wide world is "Gigi," a classic directed by Vincente. He is also responsible for many other outstanding motion pictures such as "An American in Paris," and "Lust for Life," to name a few.

This recipe is one of his favorites.

Poulet a la Minnelli

3 pound roasting chicken
¼ teaspoon salt
¼ teaspoon pepper
2 tablespoons Italian olive oil
2 tablespoons crushed rosemary leaves
1 tablespoon crushed sage leaves
2 large yellow onions
1 small garlic bud

Sprinkle chicken inside and out with salt and pepper.

Stuff with onions cut into quarters and add crushed sage leaves.

Lift skin from breast of chicken with spatula, take care not to break skin. Pour in 2 tablespoons of melted butter and crushed garlic bud. Truss chicken.

Rub skin with olive oil. Sprinkle entire chicken with crushed rosemary leaves and pepper. Half way through cooking sprinkle with salt. Place chicken, breast side up, in shallow roasting pan (just large enough to hold chicken easily.)

For basting use a small sauce pan containing 2 tablespoons unsalted butter and 1 tablespoon of Italian olive oil. Baste using a brush.

Preheat oven to 425°. Allow chicken to brown for 15 minutes. Lower over to 350°. Turn chicken on left side, basting with oil and butter. Cook for 15 minutes. Turn chicken on right side, basting with oil and butter, cook for 15 minutes. Leave chicken on its side basting every 10 minutes with pan fat.

Cooking time: 1 hour and 20 minutes.

Take chicken from oven, let stand in warm place for 10 minutes before serving. Keep covered with aluminum foil.

This was always a steady at the restaurant. It is an elegant luncheon dish and also a fantastic appetizer.

Crab Quiche

> 1 cup crab meat, flaked
> 4 eggs
> 1¾ cup half and half
> 1¼ milk
> 3 green onions, finely chopped
> salt and white pepper to taste

Use pastry dough (page 167). Combine rest of the ingredients and bake at 350° or until done, check by sticking a toothpick into quiche, if it comes out dry your quiche is done.

When I first came to California I came for only one month, to dub a movie I made in Lima in Spanish into English and I ran into John Wayne for the second time. It was at Warner Bros. Studio on his last day of work on a movie called "Trouble Along The Way" co-staring Donna Reed. (As strange as it may seem 20 years later when I first opened the restaurant I saw this beautiful woman come in with a very familiar face, we exchanged hellos and I realized who she was, Donna Reed! She is now Mrs. Grover Asmus. I am delighted to say she and her husband enjoyed the restaurant so much they became very regular customers).

Anyway, John Wayne said "I remember you, you are Pilar Pallete from Lima, Peru, how about dinner tonight?" Before I could utter a word he said "I will pick you up at 6:00 o'clock, what is your phone number?" I was thrilled. I did not know a single soul and it was Thanksgiving Day. Well, 6:00 o'clock came by and no phone call. My heart just sank. At 7:30 the telephone did ring but, it was not John Wayne, it was Mary St. John, his secretary. I thought to myself here it comes, the big excuse, she is going to tell me very politely that her boss got tied up and cannot make it. Instead, she said, "John Wayne has been nominated top box office star for the second consecutive year and has thirty reporters and newspaper people at his home for dinner and will not be able to pick you up." I said very politely thank you so much for calling, I understand." Then she said, "He has asked if it is allright with you for me to take you to his home for dinner." I said "Yes, I would be delighted!"

When we walked into his home the place looked just like a zoo. There were television cameras and newspaper people all over the place. I looked around for John Wayne but he was no place in sight.

Hampton J. Scott (affectionally called Scotty) introduced himself and said "Please come in, Mr. Wayne is looking for-ward to seeing you." (I thought to myself, then why is he not here to greet me?) I sat in a chair for what seemed eternity making small talk in my broken English and pretending I was having fun.

All of a sudden this door opened and I looked up and probably the most handsome man I have ever seen started walking towards me, I cringed and thought, he is too gorgeous, he will break your heart into a million pieces. Forget it, get out of here fast and run, now! Before I could do this he looked down at me and said, "I am so glad you could make it to share this evening with me."

Well, you guessed it, I did not go back to Lima for quite a while.

Christmas was just around the corner and I realized that Duke (notice the familiar term) loved Christmas with a passion. He decorated his home from ceiling to floor. The place was covered with tons of snow and every possible Christmas ornament, hanging not only from the Christmas tree but from every other available spot. He loved his children with a passion — and had hidden presents for them everywhere. He loved having them and his friends during the holidays.

He casually asked me, "Can you cook a turkey?" I have always heard that the way to a man's heart is through his stomach, so I immediately said "of course, I've been cooking for years". The next day, secretely I called my Mom in Lima and asked "How do you fix a Turkey?" My Mom frantically said "Oh darling, we miss you so, when are you coming home? There you are all alone in a strange country". I said "Mom, please listen to me, unless you give me that Turkey recipe I might be home tomorrow and I will probably cry steadily for a whole year!" She gave me her recipe.

So I bought this huge Turkey. The wrapper said, "Wash Turkey and pat dry." I thought to myself I better buy a brush too. And boy, did I wash that Turkey. I scrubbed it not only with water but with regular dish detergent! Duke came in just then and amazed at what I was doing said "Scotty told me he

125

would be able to spend Christmas with us and will cook the Turkey, so why don't you just relax and enjoy yourself."

Wow, what a relief!

After years of trying I now have the most delicious Turkey recipe for you.

Following is a recipe for my favorite Turkey Dressing. It can be doubled for a large bird of about 20 pounds. This recipe is for about a 10 pound bird.

It is best to order your turkey fresh as it has no sodium added to it. Wash turkey and pat dry. Do not salt. Bake at 350° for 15 minutes per pound in a grocery bag that has been greased inside with butter. Place on a rack and place the rack in a deep roasting pan. The pan will catch all the drippings. I also add water to the pan and some chopped celery, carrots, one whole large white onion, peeled, two cloves, and one bay leaf. Keep it moist by adding a glass of water to avoid pan from drying. This will make a delicious gravy.

Turkey with Dressing

1 cup finely chopped celery
½ cup finely chopped onions
1 cup bread crumbs
½ cup chopped walnuts
3 eggs
1 cup raisins
1 stick of butter, melted
   a few drops of tabasco
   salt and pepper to taste

Mix all ingredients and stuff cavity of turkey rather loosely. Dressing will expand so do not pack tightly. Be sure openings of turkey are securely sewn or laced.

After baking, remove turkey from bag and let rest on a platter for 20 minutes before carving.

Kathryn Crosby surprised me with this recipe. It was a favorite of hers and Bings.

Venison Steaks

Marinade:

Generously rub each steak with olive oil. Place in deep baking dish. Add vinegar, salt, pepper, thyme, thinly sliced onions, carrots; bay leaves, parsley and 3 or 4 juniper berries. Repeat a sprinkle of seasonings for each layer.

Add dry white or red wine as desired. Cover the baking dish and place in coldest part of refrigerator for 4 to 8 days.

Remove, wipe dry, and barbecue or grill to desired doneness.

Of all the apple pies I have had, this is my most favorite, it's incredible. It is Duke's mother's recipe. I guess he was right when he said "My mom makes the best apple pie ever." But then who's mother does not.

Apple Pie a la Mode

Make Pastry dough (page 167) and line a 9 inch pie plate with half the dough.

Pre-heat oven to 400°.

Filling:

       1 cup sugar
       1 teaspoon cinnamon
      ½ teaspoon nutmeg
      2 tablespoons flour
    2½ tablespoons butter
      8 cups green apples,
         peeled, cored, and thinly sliced

In large mixing bowl, mix the flour, sugar, cinnamon and nutmeg. Add the apples and put mixture in the pie plate, crumble the butter over apple mixture, and cover with the other half of the pastry dough. Crimp edges and brush top of pie with a mixture of 1 egg yolk mixed with a little water. Make 4 slits. Bake about 50 or 60 minutes. Serve hot with a scoop of vanilla ice cream. It can also be served cold if desired.

What a treat for your guests — a dramatic and spectacular ending to a meal.

Bananas Flambe

Serves 6

¼ lb. butter (1 stick)
6 bananas, ripe but firm
½ cup sugar
¾ cup Grand Marnier
    vanilla ice cream

In a flambe frying pan, over medium heat, melt butter until golden; add peeled bananas whole and cook them until slightly brown; turn over and repeat. Sprinkle sugar all over them, add the Grand Marnier and set fire to it immediately. Use extreme caution as flame will burst quite high so, stand far away. Shake handle of pan gently, thus moving the juice, until the flame subsides.

Arrange one banana on each plate accompanied by a scoop of ice cream. Pour some of the sauce over the ice cream.

THE HEAVENLY WORLD OF CREPES . . .

Mention the word crepes and my son Ethan comes to my mind. All my children love crepes, but Ethan can eat them as fast as I can make them.

I will always remember a Sunday when he was about 12 years old, he ask if I would fix some crepes. I said sure, and was happily at work at the stove, but everytime I looked up there was a new kid from the neighborhood, (Ethan would say, "Mom, meet so and so, and could he have a crepe, too?" Very soon there must have been twenty kids waiting in line around my stove eating crepes and syrup like there was no tomorrow. But it was worth while when one of the boys said, "Ethan was right, those things are delicious!"

Till today I always make a double batch of crepes and freeze what I do not use. I put them between wax paper in stacks of ten and seal them in foil and date them. They freeze beautifully!

There are a hundred ways to fix crepes, one better than the other. Try my Chocolate Mousse Crepes, or Manicotti Crepes, or Crepes with Smoked Salmon or the "Piece de Resistence," Caviar Crepes. Heavenly.

Basic Crepe

Approximately 30 crepes.

2 cups milk
1½ cups flour
4 eggs
  pinch of salt
  pinch of sugar
2 tablespoons melted butter

Place all ingredients in a blender and mix well.
Makes 24 crepes.

To Cook Crepes:

Let batter refrigerate for one hour. Let crepe pan heat for a few minutes. Brush the pan with oil or butter. Pour about 2 ounces of the batter into the pan. Quickly tilt the pan in all directions so as to spread the batter evenly across the bottom of the pan. As the crepe dries on the top, loosen edges and prepare to flip. When the crepe is light brown in color, flip it over and let the other side cook. Stack the cooked crepes "first" side down, as the first side to be cooked usually looks nicer than the second side. Stacking the crepes in this way will cause the nicer side to be on the outside, after rolled with a filling.

Note:
As a beginner, keep the heat on medium so as not to burn the crepes. **Also note that if you happen to own any kind of special pan for making crepes, your crepes will naturally be more beautiful than other homemade crepes.**

If you are making crepes for dessert add 1 tablespoon of sugar.

Although this is one of the most delicious sauces for a dessert, I am hesitant to give you the recipe because of an experience I once had while making it. So promise me you will work constantly with a timer while preparing it.

Caramel Sauce

In a saucepan, submerge an unopened can of sweetened condensed milk and boil it for 4 hours. The milk will turn to a thick delicious caramel. You must constantly keep checking the water to see that it has not evaporated or you will have a situation just like the one I had. I was boiling the milk and neglected to watch the water. All of a sudden, I heard this horrible explosion in the kitchen, and ran to investigate. I could not believe what I was seeing! There was caramel dripping all over the ceiling, walls and floor. There wasn't an inch that was not covered with caramel. Needless to say, we were without a kitchen for quite a while.

So please be careful to always keep the pot filled with water. After 4 hours, let the can cool overnight. After that, refrigerate until you are ready to serve it.

In a pretty, tall stem glass put a half of a canned peach; on top put a generous dollop of the caramel sauce, and top the whole thing with vanilla ice cream. Whipped cream is optional.

Caramelized Custard Molded Dessert

½ cup sugar
1 tablespoon water
2 cups milk
3 eggs
1 teaspoon vanilla

Preheat oven to 375°. Place 3 tablespoons sugar in a heavy saucepan with the water. Caramelize at high heat. Pour caramelized sugar into a one-quart mold. Make sure the caramel coats the mold.

Pour the milk into a sauce pan and bring just to the boiling point. Do not boil.

Put eggs, vanilla and remaining sugar into a bowl. Blend these ingredients. Slowly add hot milk. When blended, pour onto the caramel in the mold.

Bake mold in shallow pan containing 1½-inches of water. Place one paper towel layer in bottom of pan with water. Place mold on paper. Bake at 375° for approximately one hour.

Chill mold overnight. Unmold on platter. Garnish as desired.

The best you will ever have!

Carrot Cake with Cream Cheese Frosting

2 cups all-purpose flour
1 teaspoon baking soda
1 teaspoon salt
4 teaspoons cinnamon
2 cups sugar
1½ cups vegetable oil
4 eggs, beaten
1 small can (4 oz.) crushed pineapple, drained
3 carrots, finely grated
2½ cups walnuts, chopped

Sift together flour, baking soda, salt and cinnamon into a mixing bowl. Add sugar, oil, and eggs. Add pineapple and carrots. Grease and flour a bundt pan, large size. Pour mixture into pan and bake at 350° for 35 to 40 minutes.

Frosting:

¼ cup butter
4 oz. cream cheese
½ teaspoon vanilla
2 cups powdered sugar

In a bowl cream all ingredients together with a fork until smooth. Allow cake to cool thoroughly before frosting. If frosting is too thick, just add a few drops of milk.

Quite a treat!

Chocolate Cake with Praline

8 ounces semi-sweet chocolate
4 ounces sweet butter
5 eggs (separated)
½ cup sugar
2 tablespoons sugar for the egg whites
¼ teaspoon cream of tartar

Preheat oven to 300°. Butter and flour a 10-inch cake pan. (Recipe may be doubled to produce three 8-inch cakes.)

Melt chocolate and butter in the top of a double boiler. In a mixing bowl, combine egg yolks and ½ cup sugar. Beat well. Add melted chocolate mixture.

Beat egg whites until frothy, add cream of tartar and 2 tablespoons of sugar and beat until stiff. Gently fold chocolate mixture into whites. Pour into a pan. Bake for one hour, or until firm. Let cool ten minutes before turning out.

Praline:

1 cup heavy cream
8 ounces semi-sweet chocolate, cut into bits

Place chocolate in a heat proof bowl. In a saucepan, bring cream to a near-boil and pour over chocolate. Stir until praline is smooth and shiny.

To serve, place some praline onto a dessert plate; add a piece of the cake, top with some whipped cream mixed with Grand Marnier to taste. (optional)

Here is a recipe I received from the Princess of Wales' Lady-in-Waiting, Anne Beckwith-Smith, at Buckingham Palace, and the recipe is reproduced exactly as I received it.

I was terribly touched by her letter, not only by its promptness, but for the sincere admiration Princess Diana expressed toward John Wayne.

Chocolate Roll

English Version

   6 ounces (175 grams) plain chocolate or
      menier chocolate (Dark French Chocolate)
   5 eggs
   ½ pint (3 dl) double cream
   6 ounces (175 grams) castor sugar
   3 tablespoons hot water
      icing sugar

This recipe needs to be baked in a large, shallow tin. Use a biscuit tin approximately 13½ by 9½ inches in size.

Oil the tin and line it with a sheet of greaseproof paper. Break the chocolate into a small basin and place over a pan of hot, but not boiling, water. Stir occationally until melted. Separate the eggs. Add the sugar to the yolks and, using a wooden spoon, beat throughly until pale in colour.

When the chocolate has melted, remove from the heat and stir in the hot water — take this from the pan below the chocolate. Stir throughly until smooth, then beat the mixture into the egg yolks and sugar. Whisk the egg whites until stiff and then fold gently, but thoroughly into the chocolate mixture. Pour into the prepared tin spreading the mixture evenly. Place in the center of a moderate oven, (350° F, 180°C or Gas No. 4) and bake for 15 minutes approximately. Remove from heat, cover with a sheet of greaseproof paper and a damp cloth and leave overnight.

Turn the roll onto a sheet of greaseproof paper that has been well-dusted with icing sugar. Peel away the baking paper. Lightly whip the cream and spread evenly over the surface of the roll. Roll up like a Swiss roll using the sugared paper to help. Put to chill for several hours. When ready to serve dust the surface with a little extra sugar and using a sharp knife cut into equal size diagonals.

Here is the American version of this delightful Chocolate Roll.

> 6 ounces semi-sweet chocolate
> 5 large eggs, separated
> 1 cup heavy cream
> 6 ounces granulated sugar
> 3 tablespoons hot water
>   powdered sugar

Lightly butter a jelly roll pan which is about 13½″ by 9½″ and line it with a sheet of parchment paper. Break the chocolate into bits and place into the top of a double-boiler over hot, not boiling water. Stir until melted. Meanwhile, add fine sugar to egg yolks and beat with a whisk until pale in color. When chocolate has melted, remove from heat and stir in the hot water. Use the hot water from the bottom of the double-boiler. Stir thoroughly until smooth, then beat into the egg yolks and sugar. Beat egg whites until stiff and gently fold into the chocolate mixture. Pour into the prepared pan, spreading the mixture evenly. Bake at 350° for approximately 15 minutes. Remove from heat; cover with a sheet of parchment paper and a damp cloth and leave overnight.

Turn out the roll onto a sheet of parchment paper which has been well-dusted with powdered sugar. Peel away the parchment paper from the cake. Whip the cream until it is quite firm and spread evenly over surface of cake. Roll up the cake like a jelly roll using the sugared paper to help. Chill for several hours. When ready to serve, dust the cake with additional powdered sugar. Use a serrated bread-knife to cut into diagonal slices.

Dreamy Lemon Pie

    1 large (9-inch) baked pie shell
    4 eggs, separated
    ⅛ teaspoon salt
    1 cup sugar
    1 teaspoon butter
    2 tablespoons cold water
3 to 4 tablespoons fresh lemon juice
    1 tablespoon lemon zest

In a double boiler, combine egg yolks, salt, butter, ½ cup sugar, water, lemon juice, and lemon zest. Cook over hot water, stirring constantly until smooth and thick. Remove from heat and let stand while you beat the egg whites until stiff. Add the remaining sugar and beat thoroughly. Gradually add the lemon custard, folding until well mixed. Pour into pie shell and refrigerate until custard sets. Top with whipped cream before serving.

Note:
A meringue shell may be used instead of a pie shell.

My dear friend of many years, Dr. Miriam Wysocki, is responsible for this delicate dessert.

Chocolate Souffle (cold)

Serves 10 to 12

      2 envelopes unflavored gelatin
    2¼ cups milk
      1 cup chocolate syrup
      6 eggs, separated
      3 tablespoons butter
    1½ teaspoons vanilla
      ¼ teaspoon cream of tartar
      ¾ cup sugar
    1½ cups heavy cream, whipped
        lemon sauce (recipe follows)

Soften gelatin in ½ cup milk for 3 to 4 minutes. Set aside. Combine remaining milk, chocolate syrup, and slightly beaten egg yolks in a sauce pan. Cook and stir over medium heat until mixture just reaches boiling point. Stir in softened gelatin until dissolved. Add butter and vanilla. Cool. Cover and chill until mixture mounds when dropped from a spoon.

Beat egg whites with cream of tartar until frothy. Gradually beat in sugar, and continue to beat until mixture holds its shape.

Beat chilled gelatin mixture until smooth. Fold into meringue and blend well. Carefully fold in whipped cream. Pour into a 1-quart souffle dish with a 2-inch foil collar which has been buttered on the inside. Chill several hours. Serve with lemon sauce.

Lemon Sauce

¾ cup sugar
1½ tablespoons cornstarch
1 cup water
¼ teaspoon salt
2 tablespoons lemon juice
2 tablespoons butter or margarine
1 teaspoon grated lemon peel
dash of mace

In a saucepan combine sugar, cornstarch, water and salt. Mix well and cook over medium heat until thickened. Remove from heat and stir in lemon juice, butter or margarine, lemon peel, and mace. Chill.

Serve cold over cold chocolate souffle.

Makes 1½ cups of sauce.

Apricot Nectar Cake

1 box yellow cake mix (with pudding)
¾ cup vegetable oil
¾ cup apricot nectar
3 teaspoons lemon extract
1 teaspoon almond extract
5 eggs, separated

Mix together all ingredients, except the egg whites. Beat for 5 minutes. Then, fold in the beaten egg whites. Pour batter into a greased and floured tube cake pan and bake for 1 hour at 325°.

Icing:

Mix together ¾ cup apricot nectar and ½ cup Amaretto Liqueur. Drizzle over cake while still hot out of the oven.

CREPES

BANANAS FLAMBE

SALMON MOUSSE

SOUFFLE GRAND MARNIER

Anyone can make a scrumptious souffle, but be sure to follow certain rules.

Remove eggs from refrigerator and immediately separate, they separate better when cold, then let your egg whites stand to room temperature, they will beat bigger in volume. Be sure the egg whites have no egg yolk in them. Also the bowl you will use for the egg whites should be thoroughly clean and dry.

Use a little cream of tartar, they make the whites rise higher.

The most important part is to fold the egg whites very carefully. First mix some egg white into the base to lighten it, then you can use your hand to fold the rest.

Do not open oven door during baking.

Serve souffle immediately.

Souffle Grand Marnier

Serves 5 or 6

2	cups milk
3/4	cup sugar
1/3	cup flour
1/4	lb. unsalted butter (1 stick) softened
5	egg yolks
7	egg whites (room temperature)
1/4	teaspoon cream of tartar
2	ounces Grand Marnier

Preheat oven to 450°.

In a medium size pan, heat milk but do not boil, add sugar and stir until melted. Mix softened butter with the flour and stir into milk, blend until creamy consistency. Off the fire, add

Grand Marnier. Beat egg yolks until lemon in color and add to warm mixture, stirring continually. Let cool. In a bowl, beat egg whites; when it reaches the frothy stage, add cream of tartar and continue the beating until stiff. Pour a little of the cooled liquid at a time into the egg whites, folding very gently and continue procedure until all liquid is incorporated.

Pour into a 1½ quart Souffle dish, that has been previously buttered and sugared; put a collar of waxed paper around it.

Put in oven, reducing temperature to 400° F.

Bake for 20 to 25 minutes with oven door closed.

Just before serving, sprinkle powdered sugar over top and serve at once.

This is the sauce to end all sauces. It's the perfect topping to any dessert. My favorite!

Grand Marnier Souffle Sauce

5 egg yolks, at room temperature
½ cup powdered sugar
¼ cup Grand Marnier
1 cup heavy cream

In the top of a double-boiler, beat egg yolks until pale in color. Do not let the water in the lower part of the double-boiler reach the boiling point. Beat in the sugar, a little at a time, stirring constantly, until sugar is melted. Remove from heat and let cool. Add Grand Marnier.

In a mixing bowl, whip cream until it begins to thicken. Continue beating until peaks form. Fold into egg mixture. Refrigerate.

This divine sauce will keep for several days.

This refreshing dessert is glamorous and so easy!

Orange Baked Alaska

Serves 6

1 pint vanilla ice cream
3 large oranges
3 egg whites
¼ teaspoon cream of tartar
1/3 cup sugar
3 teaspoons Grand Marnier

Scoop ice cream into 6 balls; freeze until very firm, at least 5 hours. Cut oranges crosswise in half; cut thin slice from bottom of each so they will sit better on plates. Remove fruit and membrane from orange shells. Line bottom of each shell with orange slices and add ½ teaspoon Grand Marnier. Refrigerate.

Heat oven to 500°. Beat egg whites and cream of tartar until foamy. Beat in sugar, 1 tablespoon at a time; continue beating until stiff and glossy. Place orange cups on ungreased baking sheet; fill each cup with an ice cream ball. Completely cover ice cream with meringue, sealing it to edge of shells. Bake 2 or 3 minutes or until meringue is light brown. Serve immediately.

Coupe "Villa Fontana"

Serves 4

12 large strawberries, washed and hulled
4 tablespoons Kirschwasser
4 scoops vanilla ice cream
whipped cream

Melba Sauce:

1 pint raspberries, washed
4 tablespoons granulated sugar
4 drops red food coloring
4 tablespoons water

Wash and drain raspberries and place in saucepan. Add sugar, food coloring and water. Bring to a boil. Reduce heat and continue cooking for 5 minutes. Remove from heat and let cool. Place mixture in blender and blend until smooth. Chill.

Place vanilla ice cream in a champagne class. Put 6 half strawberries around the ice cream. Sprinkle with Kirschwasser. Pour Melba Sauce over the ice cream and top with a dollop of whipped cream.

Crepes with Chocolate Mousse

Serves 8

       6 ounces semi-sweet chocolate pieces
       1 teaspoon sugar
       1 teaspoon vanilla
    1/3 cup boiling water
       1 tablespoon cognac (optional)
       4 eggs, separated
       1 tablespoon sugar (for egg whites)
       8 dessert crepes (see page 130)

In a blender grind chocolate pieces until powdery; loosen pieces from corners so all chocolate is ground. Add sugar, vanilla, boiling water and cognac. Beat the egg whites, adding 1 tablespoon sugar when it becomes thicker and continue beating until stiff peaks are formed. Fold chocolate into whites and blend. Chill at least 1-hour before filling crepes. Divide mixture between crepes and roll. Garnish tops with whipped cream.

And then there's Maggie Glynn. If you don't have a Maggie in your life, you have not lived. It could be the rainiest, darkest day and she'll walk in and the sun will come out. You will see rainbows and hear castanets. Here is this wonderful recipe she gave me.

Flower Pot Ice Cream

1 small clay flower pot per person
  ice cream (any flavor you wish)
1 ounce semi-sweet chocolate, grated
1 fresh flower

Wash flower pot; fill with ice cream. Sprinkle on chocolate to resemble the top soil. Put into freezer until ready to serve.

Remove from freezer about 20 minutes before serving. Put any fresh flower into center and serve.

Makes a beautiful, unique dessert.

Secret Wine Cake

1 package yellow cake mix
1 package vanilla instant pudding mix
4 eggs
¾ cup dry sherry
¾ cup vegetable oil
1 level teaspoon nutmeg
½ cup chopped walnuts

Combine all ingredients. Beat for 5 minutes at medium speed, with an electric mixer. Bake in a greased angel-food pan at 325° for 45 minutes. Let cool in pan. Turn out onto a rack and sprinkle with powdered sugar.

We first had this cooling and delicious souffle at the home of Merle Oberon in Acapulco, where the weather is so hot and humid. The setting was spectacular. The tables were set on the rocks, and we could see the waves crashing all around us. Torches lit the elegant tables and provided light for the waiters to go back and forth to the main house. The dessert was certainly complementary to the tropical feeling of the evening.

Grasshopper Souffle

Serves 8

2 envelopes unflavored gelatin
1 cup cold water
1 cup sugar, divided into ½ cups
¼ teaspoon salt
6 large eggs, separated
½ cup green Creme de Menthe
½ cup white Creme de Cacao
2 cups heavy whipping cream

Sprinkle gelatin over water in a saucepan. Add ½ cup sugar, salt and egg yolks. Stir constantly over low heat until gelatin is dissolved, about 5 minutes. Remove from heat. Add Creme de Menthe and Creme de Cacao. Chill until mixture is slightly set. Place mixture into a blender or food processor and process until completely smooth. Set aside.

In a chilled bowl, whip the cream. Set aside. In another bowl, beat the egg whites with ½ cup sugar until stiff. Fold the whipped cream into the whites. Add and fold in the gelatin mixture. Pour into a 6-cup souffle dish with a 2" collar made of wax paper. This collar allows the souffle to set about ¾" above the dish. Secure the wax collar with a rubber band. Chill thoroughly for at least 2 hours.

Decorate with dollops of whipped cream and shaved chocolate.

This cake was invented by a California man, curiously enough, named Henry Baker. It was very popular for many years with Hollywood celebrities and famous restaurants. General Mills eventually bought the recipe from Mr. Baker, for an undisclosed amount, and the cake really became an all-American favorite. Of course, many variations of the cake were made. This one is my version.

Hollywood Chiffon Cake

           2 cups all-purpose flour
     1-1/3 cups sugar
           3 teaspoons baking powder
           1 teaspoon salt
       1/2 cup vegetable oil
           7 eggs, separated
             zest of one lemon, bright color (grated peel)
             zest of 1 orange, bright color (grated peel)
       1/2 teaspoon almond extract
       3/4 cup orange juice, fresh

In a mixing bowl, sift together the flour, sugar, baking powder and salt. Add the oil, egg yolks, zest of lemon and orange, almond extract and juice. Mix until batter is smooth; set it aside. Preheat oven to 325°.

Beat egg whites until they are quite stiff, but not dry. Fold whites into batter, gently, taking time to combine the two. Pour into an ungreased tube pan which is 10" x 4" (called an angel-food cake pan). Bake for 50 minutes; then increase oven heat to 350°, and bake for 15 - 20 minutes more, or until top is springy when touched. Invert pan and let cool.

To remove the cake, cut around outer edge with a knife first; then cut around the tube. Remove cake from outer form. Then carefully cut cake from bottom of tube part. Use a sharp, firm knife to remove cake from pan, such as a slicing knife.

Cake may be dusted with powdered sugar or served with a sauce, if desired.

This dessert is truly an expression of love. It says, I love you, I love you, all by itself! Prepare it for someone special in your life. I prepare it for my family occasionally and they are always so grateful.

Sheer Delight

Buy the largest green grapes you can find. Wash and peel them and remove seeds. One by one, place them into a beautiful crystal goblet; refrigerate and serve. What a treat! Low in calories, too.

This souffle is delightful!

Hot Chocolate Souffle

    4 tablespoons butter
    3 tablespoons flour (sifted all-purpose)
    2 squares unsweetened chocolate
    1 cup milk
  2/3 cup sugar
    1 teaspoon vanilla
    4 egg yolks
    6 egg whites, beaten stiffly
  1/4 teaspoon cream of tartar
      vanilla ice cream

Melt the butter in a sauce pan, remove from heat and add the flour, blend well. Melt the chocolate in the milk over low heat and add to the butter mixture. Cook over low heat until smooth, stiring constantly. Add the sugar and vanilla and keep cooking, stirring constantly. Remove from fire and cool slightly.

Beat egg yolks and add to the chocolate mixture.

Beat the egg whites, when they start to get frothy add the cream of tartar and beat until stiff. Gently fold the egg whites into the chocolate mixture.

Pour into a 6-cup greased mold. Place mold in pan of hot water and bake at 375° for 30 minutes.

Top with ice cream and serve immediately.

Pears Caramel Monaco

2 lbs. Bartlett Pears
2 cups water
  juice of 1 lemon
1 cup sugar
1 vanilla bean
1 cup heavy cream

Peal, core and quarter pears. Immediately pour lemon juice over them. In a pan, put all ingredients (except cream) and fruit, bring to a boil and continue cooking until pears are just tender, make sure you don't overcook them. Drain (keeping liquid aside) and set pears over paper toweling to absorb excess liquid. Bring remaining liquid to a rapid boil and continue cooking until liquid has been reduced to half and consistency being caramelized. Remove from heat, discard vanilla bean, and with a whisk, whip briskly while adding the cream gradually. When all of the cream has been incorporated, bring to a rapid boil again and remove from stove immediately. Arrange pears in a flat dish in one layer making sure pears are quite dry, then pour liquid mixture over them. Refrigerate overnight.

Pappy Ford was my son Ethan's Godfather, and he used to enjoy coming over to visit. He would immediately ask for Ethan. When I would bring the baby he would remove his eye patch and look at Ethan intensely, then he would turn to Duke and say, "This is a good looking baby. He doesn't look at all like his father." Pappy got a tremendous kick in teasing Duke and the feeling was mutual.

This one day I had a surprise for him, I invented an "Irish Souffle."

You will love it!

Irish Souffle

2 envelopes unflavored gelatin
1 cup cold water
1 cup sugar
6 eggs, separated
1 cup Irish liquor (Bailey's Irish Cream)
2 cups whipping cream

Sprinkle gelatin over water in a saucepan. Add ½ cup sugar and egg yolks. Stir constantly over low heat until gelatin is dissolved, about five minutes. Remove from heat. Add Bailey's Irish Cream. Chill until mixture is slightly set. Place mixture into a blender or food processor and mix until completely smooth. Set aside.

In a chilled bowl, whip the cream. Set aside. In another bowl, beat the egg whites with ½ cup sugar until stiff. Fold the whipped cream into the whites. Add and fold in the gelatin mixture. Pour into a 6-cup souffle dish with a two-inch collar made of wax paper. This collar allows the souffle to set about ¾" above the dish. Secure the wax collar with a rubber band. Chill thoroughly for at least two hours.

Decorate with dollops of whipped cream and shaved chocolate.

Kentucky Derby Tart

1 pre-baked pie crust, 9 or 10 inch
  in pan
2/3 cup sugar
4 ounces butter, cut into ½" pieces
1/2 cup all-purpose flour
2 large eggs
1/2 teaspoon lemon zest (grated peel)
1 cup dark chocolate bits
1 cup pecans
2 tablespoons bourbon

Preheat oven to 350°. Using the steel knife blade in the food processor, combine and process the sugar, butter, flour, eggs and lemon zest until smooth. Add and process for a few seconds, the chocolate bits, pecans and bourbon.

Pour mixture into 9 or 10 inch pre-baked crust (in pan) and bake for 30 minutes.

Serve at room temperature with whipped cream, if desired.

Jim Nabors is my neighbor in Honolulu, and a talented and good friend he is. His home is right in front of the blue Pacific. Palms and all kinds of lush greenery surround the property. He gave me this recipe. It is out of this world!
Hope you enjoy it.

Rainbow Torte

Serves 10 - 12

1 pint orange sherbet
1 pint raspberry sherbet
1 pint lemon or lime sherbet
2 cups crisp coconut macaroon crumbs
1/3 cup whipping cream
1/2 cup chopped macadamia nuts

Bring the sherbets to room temperature to soften slightly while preparing the crust. Set aside ½ cup of the macaroon crumbs. Stir the cream into remaining crumbs. Spread the mixture lightly over the bottom of a 9-inch cheesecake pan with removable sides. Top the crust evenly with spoonfuls of softened sherbet, alternating the three flavors to create a rainbow effect. Sprinkle the reserved crumbs and the nuts over the top, and press in gently. Cover the pan with foil and freeze until firm, at least 8 hours, or up to one week.

To serve, remove the torte from the freezer about 30 minutes before serving, and let it stand at room temperature. Remove sides of the pan and cut into wedges.

Souffle Ambrosia

with Mocha Cream

Serves 6

¼ lb. butter
½ lb. sugar
2 cups milk
1 pinch salt

Bring to a boil.

Add:

⅜ lbs. flour
2 tablespoons cocoa powder

Cook 3 minutes until it leaves side of pan.

Add 8 egg yolks, one at a time, and beat well after each yolk is added. Pour in ¼ cup Kahlua liqueur and 2 tablespoons Martell cognac and mix well.

Beat 10 egg whites until stiff — Fold ¼ of the egg white well into mixture and then fold the balance of the very stiff egg whites gently into mixture.

Butter and sugar souffle ramekins and bake in preheated oven of 425° for 20 minutes or until done. Serve immediately.

MOCHA CREAM

1 cup heavy cream, 2 tablespoons confectionary sugar. Beat until soft peaks are formed, then add 2 tablespoons of Kahlua liqueur and 1 tablespoon of Martell cognac. Beat until stiff.

This is a delightful dessert if you just want a little something sweet after dinner.

I ordered my cooking hypodermic through the mail in order to fix this luscious dessert. I waited weeks for it to arrive. I had just about given up when this little package arrived one day. I could smell it. It was my hypodermic. My thrill doubled when I opened the package and there it was. I put it in my purse and ran to the supermarket to get the biggest, most gorgeous strawberries ever. I ran to the cashier to pay for them. There was quite a crowd, so I waited patiently in line while more people lined up behind me. When my turn to pay finally arrived, I opened my purse to look for my money, and suddenly, my hypodermic fell out for the whole market to see. I looked at the crowd behind me and said, "This is to inject my strawberries with Grand Marnier." I saw twenty faces staring quizzically at my marvelous little kitchen tool, not knowing what to believe. I put my hypodermic back in my purse and walked away, feeling two inches tall. But it was worth it. It's a must for making this divine desert!

Strawberries

Covered with Chocolate

4 ounces semi-sweet chocolate
1 pint strawberries, cleaned and with stems

Inject strawberries with Grand Marnier or your choice of liqueur. Chill until good and cold.

In the top of a double-boiler with hot not boiling water melt 4-ounces of chocolate. Dip chilled berries into chocolate holding stems with fingers, dip berry top half-way. Set on an attractive serving plate.

Allow chocolate caps to chill a bit before serving.

Tomato roses are beautiful to decorate your platters and are easy to make. You need a sharp knife and a firm tomato. Just make a slit starting at the base of the tomato and keep going around the tomato cutting through the skin and meat about a half an inch deep.

Potato baskets take time but they make a meal so special. You can buy wire baskets in any specialty gourmet food shop.

These tomatoes are a compliment to any meal. You can make the stuffing the day before and refrigerate it.

Broiled Tomatoes with Ham

    6 medium firm tomatoes
    5 tablespoons chopped canned black olives
    1 cup chopped ham
    4 tablespoons chopped parsley
      mayonaise, just enough to hold the mixture
      together

Cut unpeeled tomatoes in half crosswise, scoop most of the pulp out and let them drain on a paper towel.

In a deep bowl mix the ham, olives, and parsley with the mayonnaise until well blended. Stuff the tomatoes with the ham mixture and place under broiler and broil until hot and bubbly.

Note:
Leave broiler door partially open while broiling.

Rice cooked properly was probably one of the most difficult things for me to master. I love rice and I was battling with it for the hundredth time one day when my Mom was visiting from Peru. As usual I had a terrible time with it and complained to my Mother, who said, "That's not the way to do it. Here, let me show you how." Since that day my rice has been perfect. You can actually count each grain. The kind of rice I prefer is not like Oriental rice. They fix theirs very sticky and plain.

I will never forget the first time I fixed my perfect rice. My children said they did not like it! They prefer the sticky rice, Oriental style.

Plain White Rice

2 tablespoons olive oil
2 garlic cloves, pressed
   touch of salt
2 cups water
2 cups rice thoroughly washed (very important)

In a deep pot saute garlic in oil and salt. Add water and when it boils, add the rice. Bring it to a full boil, cover and then simmer it for 20 minutes, or until cooked. Fluff the rice with a fork. You should be able to separate it easily.

C'est magnifique! This rice is always a hit. So, if you want to hear ooh's and aah's, be sure to fix it soon. It goes extremely well with chicken or beef.

Chinese Rice Peruvian Style

Begin by following the recipe for Plain White Rice on page 162. Then add:

> 5 green onions, cut very thin
> 8 pieces of bacon, fried crisp and cut fine with scissors
> 3 eggs, scrambled dry and cut into small squares
> soy sauce

Mix the onions, bacon and eggs; then mix in the rice. Add a little soy sauce and mix well.

A tangy taste to compliment any meal. Great with just about anything: beef, chicken, fish, veal, etc. . . .

Peaches and Chutney

½ peach per person

Fill canned peach-halves with chutney. Top with butter and broil until hot and bubbly.

Another delightful recipe from Jim Nabors.

Corn Bread

½ lb. yellow corn meal
½ lb. flour
1 teaspoon baking powder
3 eggs, separated
1 ounce melted butter
1 teaspoon salt
1 pint milk
½ cup boiling water

Pour boiling water over corn meal and allow it to cool completely. Beat the egg yolks and add to the cornmeal, then add the milk, flour, baking powder, salt and melted butter.

Mix well and add the egg whites (which have been beaten until very stiff.)

Pour into a shallow, well-greased, pan and bake at 375° for 25 minutes.

My dear friend Betty Godfrey served this at her home for a party — it is great!

Chile and Cheese Rice

1 cup cooked rice
1 pint sour cream
1 8-ounce can of diced green chiles
1 cup jack cheese (grated)

Combine all the ingredients and warm as a casserole.

Another one of Duke's favorites —

Hominy Grits Souffle

Serves 10

   6 cups water
1-½ cups "quick" grits
   6 ounces butter (1-½ sticks)
   1 lb. mild cheddar cheese, grated
   2 teaspoons salt
   3 eggs, beaten

In a saucepan bring the water to a boil. Add the grits and continue to boil for 10 minutes, uncovered. Remove from heat and add the butter, cheese, salt and eggs. Place in an 8 x 10 inch baking dish and bake at 350° for 1½-hours. Serve hot.

They are incredible! Her favorite.

Marisa's Potatoes

Serves 6

potatoes
heavy cream
salt
pepper

Butter a flat pan. Peel and slice potatoes round and very thin in a food processor. Put a layer of potatoes, salt and white pepper in the buttered pan. Layer three times and then cover with heavy cream. Bake at 325° for about 30 minutes or until golden.

Every since I started writing this cookbook, I have been searching for the perfect Popover recipe. After many tries, it finally happened. I turned the oven light on, and there they were . . . these huge popovers. five inches tall. I was so elated I called for the kids to come and see. My kids ran to the kitchen to see what was happening and they started hugging and kissing me, saying, "Mom, you did it!" They were aware of the time and effort I had put into this one recipe.

Popovers

Serves 6

4 eggs
2 cups milk
2 cups all-purpose enriched flour
1 teaspoon salt
½ teaspoon baking powder

First butter 10 porcelain 3-inch deep ramekins. In a deep bowl beat eggs slightly, at low speed, with an electric beater. Add remaining ingredients and continue to beat just enough to blend well. **Do not overbeat.** if batter is lumpy, put through a strainer. Fill ramekins ¾ full. Place in a cold oven; close door. Turn temperature to 425° and bake for 30 minutes. **Absolutely no peeking.** After 30 minutes turn oven off. Leave popovers in closed oven for 15 more minutes.

When done, open oven and pierce popovers with sharp knife to let out steam. This will prevent them from falling and you will not have to serve them immediately.

I use this dough for all my pies, quiches, and tarts. It is excellent to work with!

Pastry Dough

One 9 or 10 inch shell

1¼ cup all purpose flour (not sifted)
3 ounces butter (¾ stick)
1 teaspoon salt
3 tablespoons ice water (approximately)

Using a food processor with a steel blade, or a mixing bowl with a pastry blender, cut in the butter, flour, and salt until mixture resembles coarse corn meal.

Add enough cold water, a little at a time, until dough forms into a ball.

Wrap in wax paper and chill for about one hour; bring to room temperature before rolling out on a well-floured surface.

When dough has been rolled out to proper size fold it in half, and then in half again to make a quarter circle; then fit into dish and carefully unfold it. Trim excess dough. Push dough up slightly around edge of dish to about ¼" above rim. Pierce dough with fork all over; place a sheet of aluminum foil or parchment paper over dough and weight with dried beans or other weights. Bake at 450° for eight minutes. Shell is now ready to fill with whatever recipe is being used.

Mexican Corn Bread

1 cup butter
1 cup sugar
4 eggs
1 4 ounce can diced green chiles
1 lb. canned cream corn
½ cup grated Jack cheese
2 teaspoons bacon-onion seasoning
1 cup flour
1 cup cornmeal
4 teaspoons baking powder

Cream together butter and sugar. Add eggs, one at a time, mixing well after each addition. Add chiles, corn, cheese and bacon-onion seasoning; blend well.

Sift together flour, cornmeal and baking powder. Add to corn mixture and blend.

Pour into a greased and floured 12 x 8 x 2 inch baking dish. Place in a preheated oven at 350° and immediately reduce heat to 300°. Bake for one hour.

This is that divine French cream which is naturally fermented. It is used for making sauces and also served cool over fresh fruit. It is not readily available here yet, so here is the recipe. It can be made easily at home.

Creme Fraiche

Makes 3 cups

In a heavy saucepan, combine 2 cups heavy cream and 1 cup of sour cream. Stir over low heat until lukewarm.

Pour into a clean glass jar and let stand for several hours, or overnight, uncovered. Then cover the jar and refrigerate until needed. It will keep for a week.

Monkey Bread

2 ounces (½ stick) butter, melted
2 tubes refrigerator biscuits (10 per tube)

Spray a 6-cup bundt pan with butter. Separate biscuits and dip them in melted butter. Arrange in overlapping layers and bake at 375° for 30 to 40 minutes.

Note:
You can also add brown sugar and cinnamon for a sweet variation. For another scrumptious way, let your imagination run away and add walnuts, raisins or any other ingredients of your choice.

John Ford (affectionally called Pappy) was very instrumental in Duke's Career, and gave him the part of Ringo in a movie called "Stagecoach" also staring beautiful Claire Trevor. Well, the part made Duke a super star. From then on they became compadres and looked forward to working together whenever possible. They enjoyed each others company tremendously. John Ford also enjoyed the company of Ward Bond, Paul Fix, Grant Withers, Barry Fitzgerald, Pedro Armendariz, Dobe Carey and last but not least, Victor McLaglen and his son Andrew.

They were quite a wonderful rugged group of men and made many a motion picture together. Pappy also adored Ollie Carey and Maureen O'Hara who almost took my breath away the first time I ever met her, with her flaming red hair and gorgeous green eyes.

I had briefly met John Ford and his family at a Hollywood party. I immediately made friends with his daughter Barbara. Barbara's husband (then Ken Curtis) was one of the "Sons of the Pioneers" so you can just imagine what fun it was to go to their home.

I actually got to know the Fords in Honolulu, they apparently loved the place and would take their yacht the "Araner" and just settle there to their hearts desire. I could not blame them. To me Honolulu is the garden spot of the world, the lushness of the scenery, the beautiful clear warm waters, it is truly paradise. My children also adore it so we spend as much time as we can over there.

In 1954 Duke was filming a movie called "The Sea Chase" with gorgeous Lana Turner in Kona, Hawaii and John Ford was filming "Mr. Roberts" with Henry Fonda and Jack Lemon in Honolulu. Although there was a distance between the two locations they always found a way to get together, either in Kona on the big island of Hawaii or in Honolulu.

One morning just at the very end of the filming, the telephone rang, it was Duke's lawyer, Mr. Frank Belcher, to tell Duke that his divorce from his second wife had become final after a long and unpleasant court trial.

Duke ran into my room saying, "I'm free, I'm free, please marry me today."

Mary St. John. who happened to be with me at the time said "great, but we have to find her a dress." Duke came over to me and grabbed me and kissed me and said "Mrs. Wayne, you better look gorgeous tonight, and don't you forget it. You girls worry about the dress I'll take care of everything else. We're going to get married at sunset to the music of the 'Hawaiian Wedding Song' and tonight we'll fly to the Royal Hawaiian Hotel for our Honeymoon."

Mary and I dashed out of the house in search of a Wedding Dress. It was November First and I was in seventh heaven. I felt like the whole thing was a dream and I did not want to wake up. We found a lovely soft silk organza dress, and on the way home I picked some wildflowers for my hair.

The custom there was that the groom cannot see the bride until the ceremony, so I waited in my room and could hear everybody having a great deal of fun. I thought sunset was going to take an eternity that night. I could hear everyone as they gathered by the ocean, and only a big wave could quiet the laughter and talk of the people there. I also wondered who they could all be.

Finally, I heard this small knock at the door, it was John Farrow, the Director of "Sea Chase," who was going to give the bride away. John said to me, "are you ready?" I said "Oh John, I am so nervous I will probably fall right into the water, so please keep an eye on me, for I have never been happier. I love Duke so much." He said "Don't worry, I'll watch for you every second, and I know that Duke loves you very much

171

too." Then out we went, me holding on to his arm for dear life. I looked straight ahead through all of those people and saw Duke looking at me with a faint smile. All my fears dissapeared and from then on everything went smoothly and easily.

I did not realize that everyone in Kona was there. Somehow they heard about the wedding and they closed whatever businesses they were in and came to the wedding. There were hotel owners with all their personnel and each one of them brought us a dish of their choice to wish us happiness and a long life with many children.

The Hawaiian people are so dear. Duke will always live in their hearts. When I go back they always remember me and treat my children like one of their own.

The ceremony was breathtaking, we exchanged our vows just as the sun was setting. There were hues of pink, red, and lavander when we were pronounced man and wife.

The Hawaiians mixed beautifully with the cast and crew from the "Sea Chase" and danced their typical dances and played various instruments till dark.

We cut the Wedding Cake (this one recipe I did not pay much attention to.) We changed our clothes and left Kona on our way to still another small reception at the Royal Hawaiian Hotel in Honolulu.

As I am writing this book I can not help but think how everything we do is connected with food. I love the expression "Breaking Bread Together," it means friendship, love, and so many other things. Our whole lives revolve around food, and naturally you eat with the ones you love or like.

Auguste Escoffier, called "King of Chefs" and "Chef of Kings," was quoted as saying "Good cooking is the basis of true happiness."

Napoleon Bonaparte said "An army marches on it's stomach."

Marlene Dietrich was quoted saying "show me a man that had a great meal and I will show you a man that just finished a steak."

Carl Sandburg said "life is like an onion, you peel off one layer at a time . . . and sometimes you weep."

Those who indulge . . . bulge.

By the time you can afford to eat, you can't.

Never trust a skinny chef.

Orson Wells commented, "Gluttony is not a hidden vice."

Strange to see how a good dinner and feasting reconciles everybody.

Anonymous

Lettuce is like conversation, it must be fresh and crisp, so sparkling that you scarcely notice the bitter in it.

C. D. Warner

The greatest sauce is hunger.

Anonymous

The flavor of frying bacon beats orange blossoms.

P. Benjamin

173

FOR ADDITIONAL COPIES

of

Pilar Wayne's
FAVORITE AND FABULOUS
RECIPES

Contact
PAX Publishing Company
1599 Superior, Suite B
Costa Mesa, California 92627